Ghost Hunter's Guide
to
Seattle and
Puget Sound

Ghost Hunter's Guide to Seattle and Puget Sound

By Jeff Dwyer

PELICAN PUBLISHING COMPANY
GRETNA 2008

*The word "Pelican" and the depiction of a pelican
are trademarks of Pelican Publishing Company, Inc.,
and are registered in the U.S. Patent and Trademark Office.*

Library of Congress Cataloging-in-Publication Data

Dwyer, Jeff.
  Ghost hunter's guide to Seattle and Puget Sound / by Jeff Dwyer.
    p. cm.
  Includes index.
  ISBN-13: 978-1-58980-517-0 (pbk. : alk. paper) 1. Ghosts—
Washington (State)—Seattle. 2. Haunted places—Washington
(State)—Seattle. 3. Ghosts—Washington (State)—Puget Sound. 4.
Haunted places—Washington (State)—Puget Sound. I. Title.
  BF1472.U6D869 2008
  133.109797'77—dc22

                                        2008002459

Printed in the United States of America
Published by Pelican Publishing Company, Inc.
1000 Burmaster Street, Gretna, Louisiana 70053

To my son,
Michael Nicholas Dwyer,
my fearless companion on many Seattle ghost hunts

Contents

Acknowledgments

I would like to thank Sue Janet Clark for invaluable support and guidance throughout the production of this book and preceding books. Also, many thanks go to Dr. Thomas Storer, Darlene Dwyer, Marjorie Dwyer, and my friends at Pelican Publishing, Amy Kirk and John Scheyd, for their interest and encouraging messages when I needed them most. My thanks are also given to Patti Lierman of Fairhaven, Washington, for many fascinating ghost stories.

"And when the last red man shall have perished from the earth and his memory among white men shall have become a myth, these shores shall swarm with the invisible dead of my tribe, and when your children's children shall think themselves alone in the field, the store, the shop, upon the highway or in the silence of the woods they will not be alone."

—Chief Seattle, 1854

Introduction

Who believes in ghosts? People from every religion, culture, and generation believe that ghosts exist. The popularity of ghosts and haunted places in books, televisions programs, and movies reflects a belief held by many people that other dimensions and spiritual entities exist.

In 2000, a Gallup poll discovered a significant increase in the number of Americans who believe in ghosts since the question was first asked in 1978. Thirty-one percent of respondents said they believed ghosts exist. In 1978, only 11 percent admitted to believing in ghosts. Less than a year later, Gallup found that 42 percent of the public believed a house could be haunted, but only 28 percent believed that we can hear from or mentally communicate with someone who has died. A 2003 Harris poll found an astounding 51 percent of Americans believed in ghosts. As with preceding polls, belief in ghosts was greatest among women. More young people accepted the idea of ghosts than older people. Forty-four percent of people age eighteen to twenty-nine admitted a belief in ghosts compared with 13 percent of those over sixty-five. In 2005, a CBS News poll reported similar findings. Twenty-two percent of the respondents admitted they had personally seen or felt the presence of a ghost.

Today, many residents and visitors to the Seattle region believe that you can experience ghostly phenomena there. This is evidenced by the increased popularity of Seattle-area ghost tours and the number of meetings held in the Pacific Northwest region for paranormal enthusiasts. Tours of historic buildings, ships, and cemeteries around Puget Sound have become popular, too.

In October 2001, Home and Garden Television (HGTV) conducted a survey on its Web site. When asked, "Do you believe in ghosts?" 87 percent of respondents said yes. Fifty-one percent indicated they had seen a ghost, but only 38 percent would enter a haunted house alone at night.

Other cable channels have recognized the increased interest in paranormal phenomena. In the summer of 2004, the Sci Fi channel launched a weekly one-hour primetime program called *Ghost Hunters*. Sci Fi also airs programs that investigate psychic abilities, reincarnation, telekinesis, and many other fascinating topics.

NBC broadcasts a weekly primetime drama called *Medium,* which follows the true-life experiences of a psychic who communicates with ghosts in order to solve crimes. CBS joined the trend by offering another fact-based drama called *Ghost Whisperer,* which is a huge hit. The Travel Channel presents *Most Haunted* and other ghost documentaries that take viewers all over the world. In addition, more than 2.5 million references to ghosts, ghost hunting, haunted places, or related paranormal phenomena can be found on the Internet. Clearly, interest in these areas is widespread.

There is no way of knowing how many people have seen or heard a ghost only to feel too embarrassed, foolish, or frightened to admit it. Many ghost hunters and spiritual investigators believe a vast majority of people have seen or heard something from the other world but have failed to recognize it.

The recent worldwide interest in ghosts is not a spin-off of the New Age movement or the current popularity of angels or the manifestation of some new religious process. The suspicion or recognition that ghosts exist is simply the reemergence of one of mankind's oldest and most basic beliefs: there is a life after death. Ancient writings from many cultures describe apparitions and a variety of spirit manifestations that include tolling bells, chimes, disembodied crying or moaning, and whispered messages. Legends and ancient books include descriptions of ghosts, dwelling places of spirits, and periods of intense spiritual activity related to seasons or community events such as festivals or crop harvests.

Vital interactions between the living and deceased have been described. Many ancient cultures included dead people or their spirits in community life. Spirits of the dead were sought as a source of guidance, wisdom, and protection for the living. Many believers of the world's oldest religions agree that nonliving entities may be contacted for guidance or may be seen on the earthly plane. Among these are visions of saints, the Virgin Mary, and angels.

Ancient sites of intense spiritual activity in Arizona, New Mexico, and Central and South America are popular destinations for travelers seeking psychic or spiritual experiences. More modern, local sites, where a variety of paranormal events have occurred, are also popular destinations for adventurous living souls. Amateur and professional ghost hunters seek the spirits of the dearly departed in Seattle's Victorian mansions, old theaters, historic sites, and countless other places including graveyards and the famous underground city. Modern buildings, city parks, restaurants and bars, and ships, such as the Vietnam-era destroyer USS *Turner Joy* in Bremerton, also serve as targets for ghost hunters.

Throughout the past two millennia, the popularity of belief in ghosts has waxed and waned, similar to religious activity. When a rediscovery of ghosts and their role in our lives occurs, skeptics label the notion a fad or an aberration of modern lifestyles. Perhaps people are uncomfortable with the idea that ghosts exist because it involves an examination of our nature and our concepts of life, death, and after life. These concepts are most often considered in the context of religion, yet ghost hunters recognize that acceptance of the reality of ghosts and a life after death is a personal decision, having nothing to do with religious beliefs or church doctrine. An intellectual approach enables the ghost hunter to explore haunted places without religious bias or fear.

The great frequency of ghost manifestations in the Puget Sound area, as evidenced by documentary reports on TV and other news media, reflects some people's open-mindedness and wide-spread interest in ghostly experiences. Ghost hunting is becoming a weekend pastime for many adventurous souls. Advertisement of haunted inns, restaurants, and historical sites is commonplace. It is always fun, often very exciting, and may take ghost hunters places they have never dreamed of going.

ABOUT THIS BOOK

Chapter 1 of this book will help you, the ghost hunter, to research and organize your own ghost hunt. Chapters 2 through 6 describe several locations at which ghostly activity has been reported. Unlike other collections of ghost stories and descriptions of haunted places, this book emphasizes access. Addresses of each haunted site are included along with other information to assist you in locating and entering each location. Several appendices offer organizational material for your ghost hunts, including a Sighting Report Form to document your adventures, lists of suggested reading and videos, Internet resources, and organizations to contact about your experiences with ghosts.

GHOST HUNTING IN SEATTLE AND THE PUGET SOUND REGION

The very word *ghost* immediately brings to mind visions of ancient European castles, foggy moors, and dark, wind-swept ramparts where brave knights battled enemies of the crown or heroines threw themselves to their deaths. The fact is that ghosts are everywhere. A history based in antiquity that includes dark dungeons, hidden catacombs, or ancient ruins covered with a veil of sorrow and pain is not essential, but contemporary versions of these elements are common in many American cities.

Indeed, Seattle and many nearby communities have all the ingredients necessary for successful ghost hunting. Indians who inhabited the region for a thousand years or more frequently engaged in intertribal warfare while practicing a spiritual lifestyle that included communication with the dead. Since 1851, the region has been populated with people from a variety of cultures who experienced tremendous changes in their lives. These include the transitions from a wilderness to a nearly lawless American territory to admission to the Union in 1889 as the forty-second state, as well as the passage of thousands of people through the city during the Alaska gold rush of 1896-98.

Some of these changes were brought about by military campaigns, including Indian wars and skirmishes with white settlers such as the battle of January 25, 1856. Yellow fever and influenza epidemics of the 1850s and 1870s also brought tragedy to many families, ending lives at young ages and creating spirits who have yet to let go and move on.

In 1889, a catastrophic fire destroyed large portions of the city—including the business district, all the railroad terminals, and all but four wharves. Other disasters such as floods and earthquakes also played a role. Ten years earlier, a smaller but devastating fire destroyed part of the town and many wooden markers in the city cemetery. The destruction of grave markers created spiritual unrest a few years later when the cemetery was relocated. Some graves were not discovered, and the bodies were left behind to be covered by a new park and modern streets. Major earthquakes shook the region in 1949, 1965, and 2001, forcing many people to leave their homes and businesses. Some lost their lives.

All these tragic events added to the region's ghost legacy and left powerful emotional imprints created by spirits of the dearly departed who felt a need to stay on. A significant contributing factor was the loss of lives by sudden, often violent events, sometimes at young ages. These unfortunate people passed with great emotional anguish, leaving their souls with a desire to achieve their lives' objectives or with a sense of obligation to offer protection to a particular place or person. Some ghosts remain on the earthly plane for revenge or to provide guidance for someone still alive.

Seattle, Tacoma, and other Puget Sound communities have had their share of criminal activities and social injustice. The Wah Mee massacre of February 18, 1983, resulted in fourteen victims. Serial killer Ted Bundy used to stalk the Queen Anne and University districts. Even peaceful places such as the Des Moines Marina Park and Tacoma's Point Defiance Park were the scenes of tragic child murders. Years ago, the Old Pierce County Courthouse in Tacoma was the site of several hangings and prisoner suicides. On March 25, 2006, a crazed gunman shot six young people in Seattle's Capitol Hill district after an all-night party.

These events produced many used, abused, confused, and forlorn spirits who remain with us after their deaths. Their souls seek lost dreams while they remain attached to what little they gained during their difficult lives. Many ghosts who harbor resentment, pain, a sense of loss, or a desire to complete their unfinished business still roam the darkened halls of courthouses, hotels, theaters, cemeteries, modern buildings, and many other places throughout the region that are accessible to the public.

WHAT IS A GHOST?

A ghost is some aspect of the personality, spirit, consciousness, energy, mind, or soul that remains after the body dies. When any of these are detected by the living—through sight, sound, odor, or movement—the manifestation is called an apparition by parapsychologists. The rest of us call it a ghost. How the ghost manifests itself is unknown. There seems to be a close association, however, between aspects of the entity's life and its manifestation as a ghost. These include a sudden, traumatic death; strong ties to loved ones who survived the entity or a particular place; unfinished business; and strong emotions such as hatred and anger or a desire for revenge.

Ghosts differ from other paranormal phenomena by their display of intelligent action. This includes interaction with the living, performance of a purposeful activity, or a response to ongoing changes in the environment. Ghosts may speak to the living to warn of an unforeseen accident or disaster, give advice, or express their love, anger, remorse, or disappointment. They may also be trying to complete some project or duty they failed to complete before death. Some ghosts try to move furniture, room decorations, or the like to suit their preferences.

Some ghosts appear solid and function as living beings because they are unaware they are dead. Others appear as partial apparitions because they are confused about their transition from life to death. Occasionally, paranormal activity is bizarre, frightening, or dangerous. Witnesses may see objects fly about, hear strange sounds, or experience accidents. This kind of activity is attributed to a poltergeist or noisy ghost. Most authorities believe that a living person, not the dead, causes these manifestations. Generally, someone under great emotional stress releases psychic energy that creates subtle or spectacular changes in the environment.

Noises commonly associated with a poltergeist include tapping on walls or ceilings, heavy footsteps, shattered glass, ringing telephones, and running water. Objects may move about on tables or floors or fly across a room. Furniture may spin or tip over. Dangerous objects, such as knives, hammers, or pens, may hit people. These poltergeist events may last a few days, a year, or more. Discovery and removal of the emotionally unstable living person often stops the poltergeist.

HAUNTINGS

Hauntings and apparitions may not be the same thing. In fact, some professional ghost hunters and parapsychologists make a clear distinction between these two kinds of paranormal phenomena. They share a lot of the same features in terms of what witnesses see, feel, or smell, but a haunting may occur without the presence of a spiritual entity or the consciousness of a dead person. People have reported seeing pale, transparent images of the deceased walking in hallways, climbing stairs, sitting in rocking chairs, or sitting on airplanes, trains, buses, and even in restaurants. Some have been seen sleeping in beds, hanging by a rope from a tree, or walking through walls. Most commonly, a partial apparition is seen, but witnesses have reported seeing entire armies engaged in battle. Unlike ghosts, hauntings do not display intelligent action with respect to the location—they do not manipulate your new computer—and they do not interact with the living.

Hauntings may be environmental imprints or recordings or something that happened at a location as a result of the repetition of intense emotion. As such, they tend to be associated with a specific place or object, not a particular person. The ghostly figures tend to perform some kind of repetitive task or activity. Sometimes the haunting is so repetitive that witnesses feel as though they are watching a video loop that plays the same brief scene over and over. A good example is the image of a deceased grandmother who makes appearances seated in her favorite rocking chair.

There is a lot of evidence that people can trigger and experience these environmental recordings by visiting a particular site, touching an object that was a key element of the event, and psychically connecting with the event. Images of hauntings have been picked up on still and video film and in digital recordings. The location of strong environmental imprints can also be discovered through devices such as electromagnetic field detectors. Higher magnetic readings have been found at locations where psychics frequently experience hauntings.

HOW DOES A GHOST MANIFEST ITSELF?

Ghosts interact with our environment in a variety of ways that may have something to do with the strength of their personality or the level of confusion concerning their transformation by death. The talents or skills they possessed in life, their personal objectives, or their level of frustration may be their reason for trying to get our attention. Some ghosts create odors or sounds, particularly those associated with their habits, such as the smell of cigar smoke or whistling. Many reports mention the odors of tobacco, oranges, and hemp as most common. Sounds, including voice messages, may be detected with an audio recorder (see Electronic Voice Phenomenon in Chapter 1). Ghost hunters have recorded greetings, warnings, screams, sobbing, and expressions of love.

One of the most common ghostly activities is moving objects. Ghosts like to knock over stacks of cards or coins, turn doorknobs, scatter matchsticks, and move keys. For many, it appears easy to manipulate light switches and television remotes, move windows or doors, or push chairs around. Some ghosts have the power to throw objects, pull pictures from walls, or move heavy items. As a rule, ghosts cannot tolerate disturbances within the places they haunt. If you tilt a wall-mounted picture, the ghost will set it straight. Obstacles placed in the ghost's path may be pushed aside. These seemingly minor indications of ghostly activity should be recorded for future reference on the Sighting Report Form in Appendix A.

Ghosts can also create changes in the physical qualities of an environment. Ice-cold breezes and unexplained gusts of wind are often the first signs that a ghost is present. Moving or stationary cold spots, with temperatures several degrees below surrounding areas, have been detected with reliable instruments. Temperature changes sometimes occur with a feeling that the atmosphere has thickened, as if the room was suddenly filled with unseen people.

In searching for ghosts, some people use devices that detect changes in magnetic, electrical, or radio fields. However, detected changes may be subject to error, interference by other electrical devices, or misinterpretation. Measurements indicating the presence of a ghost may be difficult to capture on a permanent record.

Ghosts may create images on still cameras (film or digital) and video recorders, such as luminous fogs, balls of light called orbs, streaks of light, or the partial outline of body parts. In the 1860s, this was called spirit photography. Modern digital photographs are easily edited and make it difficult to produce convincing proof of ghostly activity.

Humanoid images are the prized objective of most ghost hunters, but they are the least to be experienced. When such images occur, they are often partial, revealing only a head and torso with an arm or two. Feet are seldom seen. Full body apparitions are extremely rare. Some ghost hunters have seen ethereal, fully transparent forms that are barely discernible. Others report seeing ghosts who appear as solid as a living being.

WHY DO GHOSTS REMAIN IN A PARTICULAR PLACE?

Ghosts remain in a particular place because they are emotionally attached to a room, building, or special surroundings that profoundly affected them during their lives or to activities or events that played a role in their deaths. A prime example is the haunted house inhabited by the ghost of a man who hanged himself in the master bedroom because his wife left him. It is widely believed that death and sudden transition from the physical world confuse a ghost. He or she remains in familiar or emotionally stabilizing surroundings to ease the strain. A place-bound ghost is most likely to occur when a violent death occurred with great emotional anguish. Ghosts may linger in a house, barn, cemetery, factory, or store waiting for a loved one or anyone familiar that might help them deal with their new level of existence. Some ghosts wander through buildings or forests, on bridges, or alongside particular sections of roads. Some await enemies, seeking revenge. Others await a friend for a chance to resolve their guilt.

UNDER WHAT CONDITIONS IS A SIGHTING MOST LIKELY?

Although ghosts may appear at any time, a sighting may occur on special holidays, anniversaries, birthdays, or during historic periods— such as July 4 or December 7— or calendar periods pertaining to the personal history of the ghost. Halloween is reputed to be a favorite night for many apparitions, while others seem to prefer their own special day or night on a weekly or monthly cycle.

Night is a traditional time for ghost activity, yet experienced ghost hunters know that sightings may occur at any time. There seems to be no consistent affinity of ghosts for darkness, but they seldom appear when artificial light is bright. Perhaps this is why ghosts shy away from camera crews and their array of lights. Ghosts seem to prefer peace and quiet, although some of them have been reported to make incessant loud sounds. Even a small group of ghost hunters may make too much noise to facilitate a sighting. For this reason, it is recommended that you limit your group to four people and oral communication be kept to a minimum.

IS GHOST HUNTING DANGEROUS?

Ghost hunting is not dangerous, but it can be frightening. Motion pictures and children's ghost stories have created a widespread notion that ghosts may inflict harm or even cause the death of people they dislike. There are a few reports of ghosts attacking people, but these are highly suspect. People who claim to have been injured by ghosts have, in most cases, precipitated the injury themselves through their own ignorance or fear. The Abbot of Trondheim ghost was reputed to have attacked some people decades ago, but circumstances and precipitating events are unclear. Authorities believe that rare attacks by ghosts are a matter of mistaken identity; that is the ghost misidentified a living person as a figure the ghost knew during its life.

It is possible that attacks may be nothing more than clumsy efforts by a ghost to achieve recognition. Witnesses of ghost appearances have found themselves in the middle of gunfights, major military battles, and other violent events yet sustained not the slightest injury. You will be safe if you keep a wary eye and a calm attitude and set aside tendencies to fear the ghost or the circumstances of its appearance.

Most authorities agree that ghosts do not travel. Ghosts will not follow you home, take up residence in your car, or attempt to occupy your body. They are held in a time and space by deep emotional ties to an event or place. Ghosts have been observed on airplanes, trains, buses, and ships. However, it is unlikely that the destination interests them. Something about the journey, some event such as a plane crash or train wreck, accounts for their appearance as travelers.

HOT SPOTS FOR GHOSTLY ACTIVITY

Numerous sites of disasters, criminal activity, suicides, devastating fires, and other tragic events abound in Seattle and the Puget Sound region, providing hundreds of opportunities for ghost hunting. Visit the locations described in Chapters 2 through 6 to experience ghostly activity discovered by others or find a hot spot to research and initiate your own ghost hunt.

Astute ghost hunters often search historical maps, drawings, and other documents to find the sites of military conflicts, buildings that no longer exist, or sites of tragic events now occupied by modern structures. For example, maps and drawings found online or displayed in museums, such as the Seattle Museum of the Mysteries, or at historic locations, such as Fort Worden in Port Townsend, may be a place to start. Doc Maynard's Public House on Pioneer Square in Seattle (entry point to the underground) and the site of the Martha Washington School for Girls on the shores of Lake Washington, may point you to the former locations of houses, bars, brothels, churches, schools, docks, logging camps, farm houses, or graves that lie under parking lots or streets. This information, which is often unpublished, may provide the key to a successful ghost hunt.

Fires and floods have caused a large number of sudden and tragic deaths in the Seattle region resulting in quite a few ghosts and hauntings. Several small-scale fires occurred in the 1860s and 1870s killing more than one hundred people and destroying wooden buildings that had been constructed with blood, sweat, and tears. In 1879, a large fire swept through the former Seattle cemetery at Denny Way and Dexter Avenue North, destroying many of the wooden grave markers. A few years later, the cemetery was relocated, but because of the lack of grave markers some bodies were left behind. People who died in these disasters and those displaced by other tragic events may haunt the site of their graves, favorite bars or restaurants, workplaces, or cherished homes.

In 1889, a huge fire swept through central Seattle, destroying hundreds of homes and businesses and killing many unfortunate souls who could not outrace the flames, smoke, or collapsing structures. The fire destroyed more than twenty-six city blocks, setting up a municipal debacle that created the famous underground city. Ghost hunters can enter Seattle's underground via Doc Maynard's Public House on Pioneer Square.

In some of Seattle's older neighborhoods, homes of many well-known residents, such as railroad magnate H. C. Henry's 1901 mansion in the Harvard-Belmont District, are reputed to harbor ghosts. Other mansions built by mayors, industrialists, judges, and timber barons that are open to the public include the H. H. Dearborn home and the C. D. Stimson mansion on Minor Street.

It has been said that all ships are haunted. Seattle has a collection of vessels that interest ghost hunters with an affinity for maritime history and sea-going spirits. At the Maritime Heritage Center on Lake Union, the 1904 vintage lightship *Swiftsure,* 1889 tugboat *Arthur Foss,* and 1897 schooner *Wawona* are open to visitors. Across Puget Sound is Bremerton, the home port of the Vietnam-era destroyer *Turner Joy.* This ship, now open to visitors, gained fame as one of two U.S. naval vessels targeted by the North Vietnamese in the Gulf of Tonkin incident.

Fascinating histories and ghostly atmospheres outside of central Seattle may be found in historic homes such as Chinaberry Hill, an 1889 Victorian inn and cottage in Tacoma; the 1900 home of John and Ida Gibson in Issaquah; and the 1887 Captain John Quincy Adams house in Port Townsend. Situated on the western shore of Puget Sound, Bremerton and Port Townsend have several historic buildings that are popular weekend destinations for ghost hunters. Access is easy because many of these places are bed-and-breakfast inns, restaurants and bars, museums, or shops.

Towns north of Seattle offer historic districts and other venues that have been investigated by professional and amateur ghost hunters. These include the Mount Baker Theatre, Bayview Cemetery, and Shuksan Rehab facility in Bellingham. Fairhaven's Sycamore Square and Patti Lierman's Off the Wall Antiques, Everett's old movie theater, and Edmonds' Anderson Cultural Arts Center are great destinations for I-5 travelers. Everett is also the home of Robert Louis Stevenson's sailing vessel *Equator* and his ghost.

For adventurous ghost hunters who don't mind a slow ferryboat ride or a hair-raising seaplane hop, the magnificent and picturesque San Juan Islands offer unique opportunities for contact with Indian spirits. At some of the resorts, inns, and restaurants on the islands, ghost hunters may encounter hauntings created by farmers and fishermen, former owners of estates, and resort patrons who came for secret rendezvous.

Many churches dating from the nineteenth century exist throughout Seattle, Tacoma, Everett, Snohomish, and Port Townsend. Some of these old places of worship include graveyards. Most of them, such as the former Methodist church on Sixteenth Street in Seattle's Capitol Hill district (now an office building) and the First Presbyterian Church on Franklin Street in Port Townsend, are beautifully restored. These churches are accessible to visitors as points of historical interest. The grounds of some of these fascinating places contain graves of well-known pioneers, in addition to mass graves of those who died in the epidemics of the nineteenth century.

Several cemeteries dating from the mid-nineteenth century are scattered about the region. Many of them have fascinating architecture, epitaphs, and lists of occupants. These cities of the dead include some unusual tombs and crypts, some marked by peculiar monuments.

Black Diamond Cemetery, located southeast of Seattle, was opened in the 1880s to serve a thriving coal-mining community. The dangerous work brought an early end to a hard life for many of the miners. On foggy nights, the lamps of long-dead coal miners can be seen as the spirits of the men walk the grounds. Some of these spirits create orbs that have been captured on film, while others whistle as they walk.

North of central Seattle in Capitol Hill, the Grand Army Cemetery houses the remains of locals who served in the Civil War, most of them in the Union Army. The adjacent Lake View Cemetery is notable for several obelisks that mark the graves of Masons. Some of these Egyptian-style monuments stand thirty feet tall and create a bizarre atmosphere. Cemeteries in Enumclaw—southeast of central Seattle—include Buckley and Evergreen Memorial Park. Local ghost hunters have conducted several investigations at these locations.

At the Western State Asylum in Steilacoom—southwest of central Seattle—more than three thousand numbered grave markers are the only monuments marking the passing of asylum inmates. These markers, about the size of a paperback novel, contain no names or dates. Visitors and ghost hunters have experienced intense paranormal phenomena there.

The best way to see Seattle's cemeteries and learn fascinating histories of those entombed there is to tour them with a knowledgeable guide. (See Appendix D.) These places are too spooky and possibly unsafe after dark unless you are accompanied by people who can insure a pleasant visit.

LOCAL GHOST HUNTERS

Two local organizations can help you locate suspected haunted sites, provide information about previous ghost investigations, and sharpen your skills as a ghost hunter.

The Washington State Ghost Hunting Society is a nonprofit organization that focuses on the scientific investigation of poltergeists, ghostly activity, and other paranormal phenomena. Many of its members are experts in physics and engineering and professionally trained in the use of audio and video equipment. Other members are talented psychics and sensitives. (See Appendix E.)

AGHOST (Amateur Ghost Hunters of Seattle-Tacoma) is considered by many to be one of the most advanced paranormal research groups in the Pacific Northwest. Its investigations have been featured on several television programs and in newspaper articles. AGHOST combines the most advanced high-tech approach to ghosts with the insight of psychics and has produced some amazing results. AGHOST conducts three to four investigations each month in apartments, hotels, open land, and at businesses and private homes. AGHOST hosts special events and offers classes and training seminars.

TWO SIMPLE RULES

Two simple rules apply for successful ghost hunting. The first is to be patient. Ghosts are everywhere, but contact may require a considerable investment of time. The second rule is to have fun.

You may report your ghost hunting experiences or suggest hot spots for ghost hunting to the author via e-mail at Ghosthunter@jeffdwyer.com.

Ghost Hunter's Guide
to
Seattle and
Puget Sound

CHAPTER 1

How to Hunt for Ghosts in Seattle

You may want to visit recognized haunted sites, listed in Chapters 2 through 6, using some of the ghost-hunting techniques described later in this chapter or you may want to conduct your own spirit investigation. If the latter is the case, choose a place you think might be haunted, like an old house in your neighborhood or a favorite bed-and-breakfast inn. You may get a lead from fascinating stories that have been passed down through your family about your ancestors.

Your search for a ghost or exploration of a haunted place starts with research. Summaries of obscure and esoteric material about possible haunted sites are available from museums, local historical societies, and bookstores. Brochures and booklets sold at historical sites, which are part of the Washington State Park system, can be good resources, too. Guided tours of historical sites, such as Seattle's underground, Pioneer Square, old churches, or fascinating cemeteries of the Puget Sound region, are good places to begin your research. Tours can help you develop a feel for places within a building where ghosts might be or an appreciation of relevant history. Seattle ghost, cemetery, and underground tours are very popular and offer a good way to learn a lot about local paranormal activity in a short time.

In addition, touring haunted buildings offers you an opportunity to speak with guides and docents who may be able to provide you with clues about the dearly departed or tell you ghost stories you won't find in published material. Docents may know people—old timers or amateur historians in the area—who can give you additional information about a site, its former owners or residents, and its potential for ghostly activity.

Almost every city has a local historical society. (See Appendix G.) These are good places to find information that may not be published anywhere else, including histories of local families and buildings; information about tragedies, disasters, or criminal activity; or legends and myths about places that may be haunted. Take note of secret scandals or other ghost-producing happenings that occurred at locations now occupied by modern buildings, roads, or parks. In these cases, someone occupying a new house or other structure could hear strange sounds, feel cold spots, or see ghosts or spirit remnants.

Newspapers are an excellent source of historical information as well. You can search for articles about ghosts, haunted places, or paranormal activity by accessing the newspaper's archives via the Internet, entering keywords, dates, or names. Newspaper articles about suicides, murders, train wrecks, plane crashes, and paranormal phenomena can often provide essential information for your ghost hunt. Stories about authentic haunted sites are common around Halloween.

Bookstores and libraries usually have special-interest sections with books on local history by local writers. A few inquiries may connect you with these authors, who may be able to help you focus your research.

If these living souls cannot help, try the dead. A visit to a local graveyard is always fruitful in identifying possible ghosts. Often, you can find headstones that indicate the person entombed died from suicide, criminal activity, a local disaster, or such. Some epitaphs may indicate if the deceased was survived by a spouse and children or died far from home.

Perhaps the best place to start a search for a ghost is within your own family. Oral histories can spark your interest in a particular ancestor, scandal, building, or site. Old photographs, death certificates, letters, wills, anniversary lists in family Bibles, and keepsakes can be great clues. Then you can visit gravesites and/or homes of your ancestors to check out the vibes as you mentally and emotionally empathize with specific aspects of your family's history.

Almost every family has a departed member who died at an early age, suffered hardships and emotional anguish, passed away suddenly due to an accident or natural disaster, or was considered a skeleton in the family's closet. Once you have focused your research on a deceased person, you need to determine if that person remains on this earthly plane as a ghost. Evaluate the individual's personal history to see if he had a reason to remain attached to a specific place.

> Was his death violent or under tragic circumstances?
> Did he die at a young age with unfinished business?
> Did the deceased leave behind loved ones who needed his support and protection?
> Was this person attached to a specific site or building?
> Would the individual be inclined to seek revenge against those responsible for his death?
> Would his devotion and sense of loyalty lead him to offer eternal companionship to loved ones?

Revenge, anger, refusal to recognize the reality of transformation by death, and other negative factors prompt many spirits to haunt places and people. However, most ghosts are motivated by positive factors. Spirits may remain at a site to offer protection to a loved one or a particular place.

Also, remember that ghosts can appear as animals or objects. By the strictest definitions, apparitions of ships, buildings, covered wagons, bridges, and roads are phantoms. A phantom is the essence of a structure that no longer exists on the physical plane. Many ghost hunters or surprised witnesses have seen houses, cottages, castles, villages, and large ships that were destroyed or sunk years before.

BASIC PREPARATION FOR GHOST HUNTING

If you decide to ghost hunt at night or on a special anniversary, make a trip to the site a few days ahead of time. During daylight hours, familiarize yourself with the place and its surroundings. Many historical sites are closed after sunset or crowded at certain times by organized tours.

TWO BASIC METHODS FOR FINDING GHOSTS

Based partly on the kind of paranormal activity reported at a site, the ghost hunter must decide which method or approach will be used. Some people feel competent with a collection of cameras, electromagnetic field detectors, digital thermometers, computers, data recorders, and other high-tech gadgets. These ghost hunters prefer to use the Technical Approach. Others may discover they have an emotional affinity for a particular historic location, a surprising fascination with an event associated with a haunting, or empathy for a deceased person. These ghost hunters may have success with the Psychic Approach. Another consideration is the ghost hunter's goal. Some desire scientific evidence of a ghost, while others simply want to experience paranormal activity.

THE TECHNICAL APPROACH

Professional ghost hunters often use an array of detection and recording devices that cover a wide range of the electromagnetic spectrum. This approach is complicated and expensive and requires technically skilled people to operate the devices. Amateur ghost hunters can get satisfying results with simple audio- and video-recording devices.

Equipment Preparation

A few days before your ghost hunt, purchase fresh film for your camera and tape for audio-recording devices. Test your batteries and bring back-up batteries and power packs with you. You should have two types of flashlights: a broad-beam light for moving around at a site and a penlight-type flashlight for narrow-field illumination while you make notes or adjust equipment. A candle is a good way to light the site in a way that is least offensive to your ghost.

Still-Photography Techniques

Many photographic techniques that work well under normal conditions are inadequate for ghost hunts, which are usually conducted under conditions of low ambient light requiring long exposures. Some investigators use a strobe or flash device, but they can make the photos look unauthentic.

Practice taking photographs with films of various light sensitivities before you go on your ghost hunt. Standard photographic films with high light sensitivity should be used. ASA of 800 or higher is recommended. At a dark or nearly dark location, mount the camera on a tripod. Try several exposure settings from one to thirty seconds and several aperture settings under various low-light conditions.

Make notes about the camera settings that work best under various light conditions. Avoid aiming the camera at a scene where there is a bright light such as a street lamp or exit sign over a doorway. These light sources may "overflow" throughout your photograph.

Some professional ghost hunters use infrared film. You should consult a professional photo-lab technician about this type of film and its associated photographic techniques. Several amateur ghost hunters use Polaroid-type cameras with interesting results. The rapid film developing system used by these cameras gives almost instant feedback about your technique and/or success in documenting ghost activities. Ghosts have reportedly written messages on Polaroid film.

Many digital cameras have features that enable automatic exposures at specific intervals, such as once every minute. This allows the ghost hunter a hands-off remote photographic record. Repetitive automatic exposures also allow a ghost hunter to investigate a site while remaining some distance away.

Your equipment should include a stable, lightweight tripod. Hand-held cameras may produce poorly focused photographs when the exposure duration is greater that $1/60$ second.

Audio-Recording Techniques

Tape recorders and digital audio recorders provide an inexpensive way to obtain evidence of ghostly activity, particularly electronic voice phenomenon or EVP. Always test your recorder under conditions you expect to find at the investigation site to reduce audio artifact and insure optimal performance of the device. If your recorder picks up excessive background noise, it may obscure ghostly sounds. Consider upgrading the tape quality and using a microphone equipped with a wind guard.

Use two or more recorders at different locations within the site. This allows you to verify sounds, such as wind against a window, and reduce the possibility of ambiguous recordings. You can use sound-activated recorders at a site overnight. They will automatically switch on whenever a sound occurs above a minimum threshold. Be aware that each sound on the tape will start with an annoying artifact, the result of a slow tape speed at the beginning of each recorded segment.

The slow tape speed could obscure the sounds made by a ghost.

Remote microphones and monitor earphones allow you to remain some distance from the site and activate the recorder when ghostly sounds are heard. If this equipment is not available, use long-play tape (sixty to ninety minutes), turn the recorder on, and let it run throughout your hunt, whether you remain stationary or walk about the site. This will provide you with a means of making audio notes rather than written notes. A head set with a microphone is especially useful with this technique.

Video Recording

Video recorders offer a wide variety of recording features from time lapse to auto start/stop, and auto focus. These features enable you to make surveillance-type recordings over many hours while you are off site. Consult your user's manual for low-light recording guidelines and always use a tripod and long-duration battery packs.

If you plan to attempt video recording, consider using two recorders, at equal distance from a specific object such as a chair. Arrange the recorders at different angles, preferably 90 degrees from each other. Another approach you might try is to use a wide-angle setting on the first camera to get a broad view of an area. On the second camera, use a close-up setting to capture ghostly apparitions at a door, chair, or window, for example.

You may have more success with sequential, manual, or timer-actuated tape runs than a continuous-record technique. If you try continuous recording, use tape runs of one to five minutes. Practice with the method that interrupts the automatic setting should you need to manually control the recording process. Always use a tripod that can be moved to a new location in a hurry.

High-Tech Equipment

Night-vision goggles can be useful in low-light situations. You can see doors and other objects move that you might not otherwise see. These goggles are quite expensive, however. You can buy devices such as electromagnetic field detectors, infrared thermometers, barometers, and motion detectors at your local electronics store or over the Internet. A good source for high-tech ghost-hunting equipment is www.technica.com. Electronic gadgets can be useful and fun, but unless you have a means of recording the output, your reports of anomalies, movements, and apparitions will not be the kind of hard evidence you need to satisfy skeptics.

Other Equipment

Various authorities in the field of ghost hunting suggest the following items to help you mark sites, detect paranormal phenomena, and collect evidence of ghostly activity:

>   White or colored chalk
>   Compass
>   Stop watch
>   Steel tape measure
>   Magnifying glass
>   First-aid kit
>   Thermometer
>   Metal detector
>   Graph paper for diagrams
>   Small mirror
>   Small bell
>   Plastic bags (for evidence)
>   Matches
>   Tape for sealing doors
>   String
>   A cross
>   A Bible
>   Cell phone

THE PSYCHIC APPROACH

The psychic approach relies upon your intuition, inner vision, or emotional connection with a deceased person, object, place, or point of time in history. You don't have to be a trained psychic to use this approach. All of us have some capacity to tap into unseen dimensions.

People who feel the peculiar atmosphere of a distant time or who believe they can perceive a voice, sound, image, touch, or texture of another dimension may have psychic abilities that will pay off in a ghost hunt. The Psychic Approach does require an ability to eliminate external and internal distractions and focus your perceptions. If you use this approach, three factors may increase your chances of experiencing ghostly activity.

The first factor is the strength of the emotional imprint or attachment the deceased has for a particular place. The frequency, duration, and consistency of the paranormal phenomena may indicate this. The strongest imprints are created by intense emotions such as fear, rage, jealously, revenge, or loss, especially if they were repetitive over long periods of time prior to death. Other emotions such as love for a person, place, or object may also create a strong imprint. Biographical research may reveal this kind of information, particularly if personal letters or diaries are examined. Old newspaper articles and photographs are useful, too.

The second factor is the degree of sensitivity the investigator has for environmental imprints. Knowledge of the key elements and historical context of the entity's death can increase your sensitivity. This includes architectural elements of a home, theater, airplane or ship, furniture, clothing, weapons, or any implement or artifact of the specific time period. Touching or handling these artifacts or standing within the historic site enables ghost hunters to get in touch with the moment of the ghost's imprint. A high degree of sensitivity for a past era often generates an odd feeling of being transported through time.

The third factor is sensitivity to or empathy for the ghost's lingering presence at a haunted site. A ghost may be trapped or confused or may have chosen to remain at a site to protect someone or guard something precious. Sensitivity for the ghost's predicament can be increased through knowledge of the entity's personal history such as emotions, motivations, problems, or unfinished business at the time of death. Research of historical sources like newspapers, old photographs, or books can provide this kind of information. Useful, intimate details might be found in letters, suicide notes, diaries, and wills.

Sensitivity to ghostly environmental imprints and spirit manifestations may be increased by meditation. This is a simple process of relaxing your physical body to eliminate distracting thoughts and tensions and achieve emotional focus. Meditation allows you to focus your spiritual awareness on a single subject: a place, entity, or historic moment in time. As the subject comes into focus, you can add information obtained from research. Markers of time or seasons, artifacts or implements, furniture, and doorways are a few suggestions. By doing this, you become aware of unseen dimensions of the world around you that create a feeling that you have moved through time to a distant era. This process gets you in touch with the place, date, and time pertinent to a ghost's imprint or death. The process also enables you to disregard personal concerns and distracting thoughts that may interfere with your concentration on the ghost you seek.

Keep in mind that it is possible to be in a meditative "state" while appearing quite normal. The process is simple and easy to learn. When you arrive at the site of your ghost hunt, find a place a short distance away to meditate. Three essentials for any effective meditation are comfort, quiet, and concentration.

Comfort: Sit or stand in a relaxed position. Take free and even breaths at a slow rate. Do not alter your breathing pattern so much that you feel short of breath, winded, or lightheaded. Close your eyes if that enhances your comfort or focus on a candle, tree, or flower. Do not fall asleep. Proper meditation creates relaxation without decreasing alertness.

Quiet: Meditate in a place away from noises generated by traffic, passersby, radios, slammed doors, and the like. If you are with a group, give each other sufficient personal space. Some people use mantras or repetitive words or phrases; others speak only in their mind in order to facilitate inner calmness.

Mantras are useful to induce a focused state of relaxation, but they may disrupt the meditation of a companion if spoken aloud. A majority of ghost hunters do not believe that mantras are necessary in this instance. They point out that ghost hunting is not like a séance as depicted in old movies. It is not necessary to chant special words, call out to the dead, or invite an appearance from beyond the grave.

Concentration: Clear your mind of everyday thoughts, worries, and concerns. This is the most difficult part of the process. Many people don't want to let go of their stressful thoughts. To help you let go of those thoughts, let the thought turn off its light and fade into darkness. After you clear your mind, some thoughts may reappear. Repeat the process. Slowly turn off the light of each thought until you can rest with a completely clear mind. This might take some practice. Don't wait until you are on the scene of a ghost hunt before you practice this exercise.

Once your mind is clear, focus on your breathing and imagine your entire being as a single point of energy driving the breathing process. Then, open yourself, thinking only of the entity you seek. Starting with the ghost's identity (if known), slowly expand your focus to include its personal history, the historical era of the ghost's death or creation of the emotional imprint, the reported nature and appearance of the haunting, or any specific ghostly activity.

Acknowledge each thought as you continue relaxed breathing. Find a thought that is most attractive to you, and then expand your mind to include your present surroundings. Return slowly to your current place and time. Remain quiet for a minute or two before you resume communication with your companions, then move ahead with the ghost hunt.

GROUP ORGANIZATION AND PREPARATION

It is not necessary to be a believer in spirits or paranormal phenomena in order to see a ghost or experience haunting activities. Indeed, most reports of ghost activities are made by unsuspecting people who never gave the matter much thought. But you should not include people in your group with openly negative attitudes about these things. If you include skeptics, be sure they maintain an open mind and are willing to participate in a positive group attitude.

Keep your group small, limited to four members if possible. Ghosts have been seen by large groups of people, but small groups are more easily managed and likely to be of one mind in terms of objectives and methods.

Meet an hour or more prior to starting the ghost hunt at a location away from the site. Review the history of the ghost you seek and the previous reports of ghost activity at the site. Discuss the group's expectations based on known or suspected ghostly activity or specific research goals. Review possible audio and visual apparitions based on the history of paranormal activity at the site, telekinesis, local temperature changes, and intended methods of identifying or recording these phenomena. Most important, agree to a plan of action if a sighting is made by any member of the group.

The first priority for a ghost hunter is to maintain visual or auditory contact without a lot of activity such as making notes. Without breaking contact, do the following:

- activate recording devices
- redirect audio, video, or photographic equipment to focus on the ghost
- move to the most advantageous position for listening or viewing the ghostly activity
- attract the attention of group members with a code word, hand signal (touch the top of your head), or any action that signals other hunters so they can pick up your focus of attention

Only attempt to interact with the ghost if it invites you to speak or move. Often, ghost hunters' movements or noises frighten the ghost or interfere with the perception of the apparition.

SEARCHING FOR GHOSTS

There are no strict rules or guidelines for successful ghost hunting except to be patient. Professional ghost hunters sometimes wait several days, weeks, or even months before achieving contact with a ghost. Others have observed full-body apparitions when they least expected it, while concentrating fully on some other activity. Regardless of the depth of your research or preparation, you need to be patient. The serious ghost hunter should anticipate that several trips to a haunted site may be required before some sign of ghostly activity is observed.

If you hunt with a group, you need to establish a communications system in the event that one member sights a ghost or experiences some evidence of ghostly activity. Of course, confirmation by a second person is important in establishing validity and credibility. In the previous section, a hand signal (hand to the top of the head) was recommended as a means of informing others that they should direct their eyes and ears to a site indicated by the person in contact with a ghost. Because of this, all ghost hunters need to keep their companions in sight at all times and be aware of hand signals.

An audio signal can often reduce the need for monitoring other ghost hunters for hand signals. Equally important for a group is to establish a method for calling other hunters who may be some distance away. Tugging on a length of string can be an effective signal, as can beeping devices, mechanical "crickets," and flashing penlight signals, such as one flash for a cold spot and two flashes for an apparition. Hand-held radios, or walkie-talkies, can also be effective. Some models can send an audio signal or activate flashing lights. Cell phones can be used, but the electromagnetic activity may be uninviting to your ghost.

Remaining stationary within a room, at a gravesite, courtyard, or other confirmed location is often most productive. If a ghost is known to have a favorite chair, bed, or other place within a room, it will appear. Under these conditions, the patient ghost hunter will have a successful hunt.

If the ghost is not known to appear at a specific place within a room or an outdoors area, take a position that allows the broadest view of the site. A corner of a room is optimal because it allows the ghost unobstructed motion about the place while avoiding the impression of a trap set by uninvited people who occupy the ghost's favorite space. If you are outdoors at a gravesite, for instance, position yourself at the base of a tree or in the shadows of a monument to conceal your presence while affording a view of your ghost's grave.

If your ghost is a mobile spirit, moving throughout a house, over a bridge, or about a courtyard or graveyard, you may have no choice but to move around the area. Search for a place where you feel a change in the thickness of the air, a cold spot, or detect a peculiar odor.

If you are ghost hunting with others, it may be advantageous to station members of your group at various places in the ghost's haunting grounds and use a reliable system to alert others to spirit activity. Each member could then patrol a portion of the site. Radio or cell-phone communications may be essential for this type of ghost hunt.

Once you are on site, the above-described meditation may help you focus and maintain empathy for your ghost. Investigate sounds, even common sounds, as the ghost attempts to communicate with you. Make mental notes of the room temperature, air movement, and any sensations of abrupt change in atmosphere as you move about the site. Changes in these factors may indicate the presence of a ghost.

Pay attention to your own sensations or perceptions, such as the odd feeling that someone is watching you, standing close by, or touching you. Your ghost may be hunting you!

WHAT TO DO WITH A GHOST

On occasion, professional ghost hunters make contact with a ghost by entering a trance and establishing two-way communications. The ghost hunter's companions hear him or her speak but the ghost's voice can only be heard by the trance communicator. Sylvia Browne's book *Adventures of a Psychic* describes several of these trance communication sessions. However, most ghost encounters are brief, with little opportunity to engage the entity in conversation. But the ghost may make gestures or acknowledge your presence through eye contact, a touch on the shoulder, sound, or a movement of an object. The ghost hunter must decide whether to follow the gestures or direction of a ghost.

Visitors to Seattle's historic buildings, Victorian mansions, and churches often feel the touch or tug of ghosts on their arms or shoulders. These may be the actions of ghosts trying to get living souls to notice them, move out of their way, or follow them to some important destination.

A ghost at Point Wilson lighthouse in Port Townsend points to a location offshore that may be the site of a shipwreck or where he lost his life by drowning. Ghosts who wander the islands of Puget Sound sometimes wave to people hiking the trails or passing by on ferryboats, beckoning the people to follow.

The ghost of a little girl at Des Moines Marina Park may want you to give her a gentle push as she continues her swinging. Spirits at the Varsity Theatre or Harvard Exit Theatre in Seattle may try to attract attention to get people out of their way as they move to a favorite seat. Patrons who dine at E. R. Rogers restaurant in Steilacoom, the Starlight Lounge in downtown Seattle, or even the Pike Place Public Market may get a glimpse of spirits who still wander the old city more than 150 years after their deaths.

People who are brave enough to tour Seattle's underground city may hear the voices and revelry of long-deceased barmaids, prostitutes, hard-drinking sailors, or dock workers. These lost souls may touch you, stir the air, or give you a chill as they try to attract your attention. They may want you to show them the way out of this strange, dark subterranean city or follow them to a secret lair.

While crossing the Heart Bridge in Seattle's Kubota Gardens, visitors may feel the rush of several male ghosts as they race across the picturesque bridge. In Maynard Alley in downtown Seattle, emotional residue and other ghostly phenomena resulting from the Wah Mee Massacre of 1983 affects sensitive visitors, creating a sensation of being pulled downward. Some feel environmental imprints left by the murderers, while other lucky visitors have seen ghosts of the fourteen murder victims.

To date, there are no reports of lasting ill effects on those who have been brave enough to follow these spirits or experienced contact with them. Experience with an unfriendly ghost can be disturbing. It may be time to leave when you have established the nature of the ghost activity, ascertained that your companions have experienced the activity, made a few photographs, and run a few minutes of audio tape. Often, the ghost's activities are directed at getting the intruder to leave a room, house, or gravesite. If you sense that your ghost wants you to leave, most ghost hunters believe it is best not to push your luck.

Residents of haunted houses and employees of haunted business establishments often accept the ghost's telekinetic or audio activities without concern. It is part of the charm of a place and may add some fun to working in a spooky building.

AFTER THE GHOST HUNT

Turn off all recorders and remove them to a safe place. Some ghost hunters suspect that ghosts can erase tapes. Label your tapes with the date, time, and location. Use a code number for each tape. Keep a separate record of where the tape was made, as well as the date, time, and contents. Place tapes in a water-proof bag with your name, address, telephone number, and a note that guarantees postage in case it is misplaced.

Have photographic film developed at a professional color laboratory.

Pros at the lab may help you with cropping and image enhancement. Have copies made of any negatives that contain ghostly images.

All members of the group should meet right after the hunt away from the site. Each hunter who witnessed ghostly activity or an apparition should make a written or audio statement describing the experience. The Sighting Report Form presented in Appendix A is for the group leader to complete. Video and audio recordings made at the site should be reviewed and reconciled with witness statements. Then, plans should be made for a follow-up site visit in the near future to confirm the apparition, its nature and form, and the impressions of the initial ghost hunt.

Data about the ghost's location within a site may indicate the optimal conditions for future contact. Things to be aware of include the time of day or night, phase of the moon, season, temperature and size of cold spots, as well as form and density of the apparition. Patience and detailed records can help you to achieve the greatest reward for a ghost hunter—unmistakable proof of ghostly activity.

CHAPTER 2

Western Puget Sound Communities

The western side of Puget Sound offers some of this most beautiful scenery and fascinating history in the Pacific Northwest. A one-hour ferryboat passage from Seattle gets you to Bremerton and from there Gig Harbor, Port Townsend, and many other interesting hamlets that offer opportunities for ghost hunters. Destinations such as Port Townsend can be a day-trip for Seattle residents and visitors, but the haunted locations will entice you to stay a few days.

MANRESA CASTLE

651 Cleveland Street
Port Townsend 98368
460-385-5883 or 800-732-1281
www.manresacastle.com

Manresa Castle may be one of the most haunted buildings in America. Approaching the place late in the afternoon under an overcast sky, visitors might get that weak-in-the-knees feeling and ask, "Do we really want to spend a night in this place?" The grounds are beautiful, the parking lot spacious, and the exterior in excellent condition. But the tall turret with conical roof and heavy doors at the top of the stairs tells visitors this may offer something far beyond the usual weekend retreat.

I spent a night completely alone in the most haunted room of the castle, number 306. Afterward, I decided that the Manresa Castle matched the most haunted house in America—the famous Myrtles

Built in 1892, Manresa Castle overlooks Port Townsend and harbors at least two ghosts.

Plantation in Louisiana—for ghostly activity. The Port Townsend landmark also has a fascinating history with many ghost reports, magnificent architectural features, an excellent restaurant and bar, and a staff who can make ghost hunting an unforgettable experience. Ghost hunters traveling the Puget Sound area should place this location at the very top of their list of must-see haunted sites.

The castle was built in 1892 by Port Townsend's first mayor, Charles Eisenbeis. Having amassed a fortune in several businesses, including the manufacture of bricks, lumber, and banking, Eisenbeis built the largest private residence in town using bricks from his own factory. With thirty rooms and four floors, Eisenbeis designed his home so it would resemble castles in his native Prussia. Charles and his wife, Kate, entertained the upper crust of Port Townsend society in high style until his death in 1902.

Kate remained in the house until 1906, then moved out and remarried. The Eisenbeis Castle was left vacant except for a solitary caretaker for twenty years and then sold to the Jesuits in 1927. The holy order made several modifications and added a west wing, converting the mansion to dormitories and a seminary. They called the place Manresa Hall after the city in Spain where their order was founded. The seminary closed in 1968 and soon became a hotel. To meet modern standards, the owners added forty bathrooms, but the charm of the original woodwork, Victorian furnishings, and the elegant lifestyle of the Eisenbeises were preserved. As a tribute to the builder and the Jesuits, the place was called Manresa Castle.

For visitors walking through the hallways late in the evening, the dim light, century-old wall coverings, ornate woodwork, and old doorknobs give the impression that elegant gentlemen and ladies, dressed in Victorian attire, might appear at any moment. In fact, sensitive people on the lookout for ghosts might see that very thing. Manresa Castle probably is home to several ghosts, including that of Charles Eisenbeis, but the castle is best known for two particular spirits.

In the early 1930s, a young Jesuit in training committed suicide in the attic. A rumor started that the distraught fellow had violated the code of behavior by having unsupervised visits with a nun who resided in town. Unable to come to grips with his emotions and hormones, he climbed to the attic one night and hanged himself from the rafters that support the turret. Often, third-floor guests report hearing a rope stretching and the beams groaning as if a body is swinging in the darkness of the huge attic.

The attic is off limits to guests, but hotel staff might allow a brief visit if you explain your purpose. I visited the attic after 11:00 on a winter night and discovered a hangman's noose still hanging from a beam. The night-desk manager who accompanied me explained that the noose was a prop left by a film crew that had visited the castle only a week earlier. As I watched, the noose began to swing through an eighteen-inch arc. The beam from which the rope was suspended creaked and groaned as if a heavy weight were suspended from it.

A better-known and much more active ghost is that of a young woman named Kate or Katie. This woman was not Kate Eisenbeis, but a guest in the castle who spent several months in room 306 after Charles' death in 1902. This ghost responds to Kate, Katie, and Katherine, and she doesn't like being reminded that she committed suicide.

The story is that Kate stayed at the castle waiting for her fiancé to return from a long voyage on a merchant ship. One day she received news that the ship had sunk in a storm in the Bering Sea. Distraught, Kate threw herself from one of the windows of room 306 and died when she hit the paved walk below. The tragedy became legendary when Kate's young man returned to Port Townsend after being rescued by a passing ship.

This story plays out like the stereotypical tragedy of a lonely woman who could not bear to live without her lover. My recent investigation, however, turned up another interesting possibility. The ghost of Kate was provoked into making an appearance in room 306 by a technique seldom used by ghost hunters. I used derogatory accusations, insults, and challenges all built around words that cannot be included in this book. All of this made Kate angry and gave me one of the longest spirit contacts and bizarre nights I have ever known.

Kate started by creating the odor of spoiled meat at the threshold of room 306. Stepping through it, in either direction, was nauseating. She also created intense cold in the bathroom, walked over the bedding as I lay in bed, tugged at the blankets, and changed the thermostat from very cold to hot. Kate's pale image also appeared several times, reflected in a window as she faced outward re-creating the final moment before she jumped to her death. She appeared to be short and slender, with long, light-colored hair. (The portrait in the bar of a young woman is believed to be the suicidal Kate.)

The angry Kate kept me awake most of the night with her antics and left some amazing impressions. By verbal and psychic communication,

This portrait hangs in the bar at Manresa Castle. It may be of a woman named Kate, who still haunts room 306.

Kate revealed that she was not faithful to her fiancé while he was away on the long and fateful voyage to Alaska. She had, in fact, become pregnant while he was gone. After agonizing weeks of mourning after the news of his death, Kate became guilt ridden because of her infidelity when she learned her fiancé had been saved and was on his way to Port Townsend. Unable to face him, she ended her life on the walk in front of the Eisenbeis castle.

After so many wild nights of Kate's ghostly antics, it is not surprising that a comment book kept in room 306 for guests was removed a few years ago. So many bizarre and frightening entries had been made that, after reading them, many guests became too nervous to sleep and asked for different rooms.

The ghost of Kate Eisenbeis is believed to haunt the castle mansion as well. I captured a digital image of a lady in a long Victorian gown sitting at a table in the dining room. The lady may be Kate or one of the many guests at the frequent social events hosted by the Eisenbeis family. Guests and staff have reported chimes from a broken clock in the library across the entry from the castle's front desk and disembodied singing. The library was once the choir loft overlooking the Jesuit chapel, which now serves as the breakfast room. Throughout the castle, doors open and close by themselves, lights go on and off, blankets are tugged off sleeping guests, and unexplained puffs of air pass over visitors' shoulders as they walk down darkened hallways.

HOLLY HILL HOUSE BED-AND-BREAKFAST

611 Polk Street
Port Townsend 99368
360-385-5619 or 800-435-1454
www.hollyhillhouse.com

"I know what people say. But there aren't any ghosts here," proprietor Nina Dortch told me. "At least I've never seen anything odd."

Dortch was sincere, but the historic Holly Hill House has all the elements for a haunting. Many visitors, ghost hunters, and weekend vacationers have reported ghostly phenomena.

The Holly Hill House stands in Victorian splendor on a large corner lot at Polk and Clay streets. Built in 1872 by J. J. Hunt, its first occupants were Robert and Elizabeth Hill, who took up residence in 1881. They filled the place with all the comforts moderate wealth could provide, plus three children. Today, the house is a popular bed-and-breakfast inn that offers guests the experience of a beautifully

Holly Hill House may harbor the ghost of a Port Townsend mayor.

restored Victorian home surrounded by delightful gardens that contain 185 rose bushes. Furnishings are true to the house's period with
the interesting exception of aviation sculpture, artifacts, and prints—
some signed by famous aviators—that adorn the parlor.

Several reports of ghostly encounters at Holly Hill House, some by
AGHOST members, include the sound of a piano, but one does not
exist in the house. Others report the odor of cigar smoke and an
apparition of a man dressed in early-twentieth-century clothing.
These experiences, together with the history of the Hill family, suggest that Robert Crosby Hill or his son William is the specter that
roams the narrows halls of this home.

Soon after moving into the house, Robert and Elizabeth produced
three sons, Horace, William, and Harry, step-brothers to Elizabeth's
son, Albert, by a previous marriage. Even with a busy household to
run, Elizabeth was a popular hostess, often entertaining the upper
crust of Port Townsend's feminine society. It is likely that her social
events included piano recitals.

Robert became prominent in the banking industry and served a term as mayor. He died May 11, 1916, in an upstairs bedroom. It is no surprise that cigar smoke has been detected in that room. Elizabeth died on December 1, 1919.

The Hills' son William, also known as Billie, remained in Port Townsend, achieved success in many enterprises, and became a community leader of sorts. His greatest public event was to deliver the Fourth of July speech in 1937. Unfortunately, while speaking to that huge gathering, he suffered a stroke. His wife, Lizette, converted the lady's parlor (to the right of the entry; now used as an office and library) to a bedroom complete with the most modern furniture and equipment for Billie's convalescence. It is doubtful that he ever regained enough strength to leave the room. Billie died New Year's Eve 1937.

The apparition of a man, either Billie or his father, Robert, has been seen on the stairs and in the room in which Billie died. The odor of cigar smoke experienced by several visitors has most often been detected in the upstairs bedroom facing Polk Street, where Robert took his last breath. The soft notes of a piano have been heard in the office/library, dining room, and parlor. Once the lady's parlor, this room would have been the site of Elizabeth's social gatherings.

The presence of a female spirit has been detected at various places in the house and in the yards. It might be Lizette, still looking after her bed-ridden husband, or Elizabeth Hill, who simply cannot leave her magnificent gardens.

POINT WILSON LIGHTHOUSE

Fort Worden State Park
Port Townsend 98368
206-457-4401
www.ptguide.com/history/sites/l_pwlighthouse.html

There is something about old lighthouses that is alluring, fascinating, and spooky. Most of them stand at remote locations, marking a dangerous point of land, hazardous coastline, or treacherous harbor entrance. Inquiries into the history of any lighthouse will turn up more than a few tragic events such as shipwrecks, drownings, and

Several maritime disasters have taken place near Point Wilson Lighthouse.

other disasters. Added to these stories are common tales of lonely light keepers, or wives of light keepers, who killed themselves. Some wandered off cliffs in a thick fog, while others died by falling down winding stairs. Point Wilson Lighthouse, near Port Townsend, has some of these elements in its history, so a few ghosts may stand watch in the light tower and wander the grounds.

Point Wilson Lighthouse was established in 1879 to mark a major point of navigation—where the Strait of Juan de Fuca joins Admiralty Inlet—for ships entering Puget Sound. Ships rounding this point must make a sharp turn southward before the shipping channel narrows. Frequent fog added to the hazards of the area, but the Point Wilson light averted many disasters.

In 1904, a storm struck the point, driving high tides over the rocky shore and damaging the lighthouse. There is no official record of lives lost during this storm, but local legend tells of two men who were washed away as they tried to secure a boat behind the huge boulders that form a seawall. Shipping disasters and other tragic events may have also created environmental imprints and entrapped spirits, which may be found near the boulders guarding the lighthouse from the treacherous sea. Sensitive visitors who walk the boulders may encounter cold spots that cannot be explained by environmental factors. Visitors who arrive here at sunset may see strange lights, reminiscent of hand-held lanterns, moving along the shore.

Point Wilson Lighthouse is open for tours by special arrangement with the Coast Guard. Docents tell tales of lonely watches kept for years by dedicated light keepers, phantom ships, and stories about the people who lived at this Puget Sound outpost.

ALEXANDER'S CASTLE

Fort Worden State Park
Port Townsend 98368
360-344-4400
www.parks.wa.gov/fortworden/

John Alexander arrived in Port Townsend in 1882 to assume the rector duties of St. Paul's Episcopal Church. That same year, he purchased a lot a few miles from town on land that would later become Fort Worden. At the time, the acreage was remote, but it offered spectacular views of Puget Sound as well as lush pastures for sheep and goats. With his mind on the future, Alexander immediately began to build a solid brick home reminiscent of his native Scotland. With firm walls and small windows to keep out the cold, damp air, Alexander was certain it would please the woman he loved who waited for him in Scotland. He

Alexander's Castle at Fort Worden was the home of a lonely bachelor who now haunts the place.

even added a three-story tower, with ramparts similar to those of a medieval castle. The tower provided two rooms with views of the sound. The roof was designed to catch and store rain water, which provided a system of running water for the kitchen and bathroom.

Pleased with his new home, John Alexander sailed for Scotland to claim his bride. But after many weeks at sea, he arrived only to learn that she had already married. Apparently, the years Alexander spent thousands of miles away building a home and establishing his career led the young lady to seek companionship among the men of her town. Alexander returned to Port Townsend and probably faced a good deal of embarrassment, as his parishioners expected to meet Mrs. Alexander and welcome her to the community.

Alexander continued to serve as rector of St. Paul's, but led a solitary life in his remote home. Finally, in 1892, Alexander left Port Townsend to take a position in Tacoma as Her Majesty's consul in the Puget Sound region. He died there in 1930, unmarried.

John Alexander's castle stood vacant until Fort Worden was constructed in 1897. The fine brick house served as a tailor shop, artillery observation platform, and residence for officers. Today, it stands nicely preserved as a monument to a man whose greatest dream was never fulfilled.

Members of AGHOST have visited Alexander's Castle several times. They have reported orbs captured on film and ghostly sounds emanating from the vacant house. I visited the place late in the afternoon with no other visitors nearby. Pressing my ear to the window of the south-facing door, I heard the sound of heavy footsteps. I also detected a clanking sound, as if unseen hands were slamming the door of a cast-iron stove.

The sad story of John Alexander, living alone during the years following his great disappointment and deep emotional wound, points to the conclusion that strong environmental imprints, created by depression and longing, remain at this site.

MILITARY GHOSTS OF FORT WORDEN STATE PARK

Port Townsend 98368
360-344-4400
www.parks.wa.gov/fortworden

Fort Worden may be one of the most haunted places in the Seattle region. Established for coastal defense in 1889, the fort sits on the outskirts of Port Townsend and covers 433 acres. The military moved out in the 1950s and transferred the facilities to the Washington State

Once the home of Fort Worden's commanding officers, this mansion emits ghostly odors.

Park system. The park offers campgrounds, dormitories for meetings and retreats, miles of hiking trails, hostels, conference rooms, several points of historical interest, and fishing and boating facilities. More than fifty of the original buildings still stand, most of them well-pre-served as excellent examples of military architecture. Among them are officers' quarters that resemble Victorian mansions, a guard house, and enlisted men's barracks. The fort also includes a cemetery, gun emplacements, and parade ground. The grounds are open to the public during daylight hours, and many ghost hunts have achieved success even on sunny days. Access at night is limited. Contact the park manager for a permit for night visitation. For ghost hunts at night, you should also contact AGHOST or other tour organizations.

The parade grounds dominate Fort Worden. Covering more than fifteen acres and terminating on the eastern border of the fort, the grounds lay in front of officers' row, a line of large houses that were provided for the commanders and their families. Several ghost hunters have captured orbs floating over the parade grounds using film and digital media. Ghost hunter Fiona Broome posted some of her orb images on www.hollowhill.com. She also described "sparkles" or splinters of light that cannot be captured photographically. Broome interpreted these visual experiences as an indication that paranormal activity is occurring.

While walking over the parade ground late in the afternoon, I encountered a small area, or cell, in which the odor of cigar smoke was intense. The cell was about five feet in diameter and extended from a point three feet above ground to about seven feet. The site was about one hundred feet from the eastern boundary of the parade grounds, midway from the side boundaries. At the time of this encounter, there was no wind nor were any people walking on the grounds. This phenomenon may signal the presence of a soldier, officer, or non-commissioned officer, such as a sergeant major. Lower-rank enlisted soldiers would not have had the privilege of smoking on the parade grounds.

A long row of officers' mansions sits on Pershing Avenue overlooking the parade ground. Many of these have been investigated by ghost hunters. Quarters for the fort's commanding officer sit at the east end of the avenue, providing a view of Admiralty Inlet. The home, named for Colonel Clarence Deems, is haunted by a former occupant. A photograph of the apparition was published in the Port Townsend *Leader* newspaper in August 2005. Others have detected the strong odor of burning coal, burning rubber, and hot sulfur near the main entrance. It is likely that a fire broke out in this house, possibly a result of a faulty coal-burning stove. These odors have been detected by sensitive visitors standing on the front porch.

The military cemetery at Fort Worden has been the scene of many ghost hunts.

Other homes and dormitories, believed to be haunted, include Buildings 11W and 5W, both former officers' quarters, and Building 201. The latter served as a Washington state reform school from 1950 to the early 1970s. Detention cells used for violent and incorrigible inmates are believed to harbor several ghosts.

On the west side of Fort Worden sits a military cemetery. Neat rows of headstones engraved with name, rank, military unit, and dates stand among closely cropped grass. A monument topped by cannon sits in the center of the cemetery. A small caretaker's garage can be found along the north fence. Ghost hunters may feel the peculiar vibes generated by so many graves placed so closely together, but there are no reports of apparitions appearing here. EVP documentation may be fruitful, and orbs have been captured in photographs.

The woods that stand along the north border of the cemetery, however, do seem haunted. Even under the light of the midday sun, the woods have spooky shadows and peculiar cold spots. On entering the woods, I encountered a chilling atmosphere and perceived a dark foreboding, as if something terrible happened there. The negative energy remains as a strong environmental imprint. My EVP equipment would not function during this brief experience.

A hot spot for ghostly activity, including orbs and other visual phenomena, is the guard house on Battery Way. The building now serves as the information center and gift shop, but it was once the scene of harsh discipline dispensed by military police and guards. The toughest of the tough comprised the military police. Well armed and highly trained, they meted out discipline and filled the detention cells in the basement. Most of the soldiers there reeled from a wild night on the town that might have included a barroom brawl and a rap on the head by a night stick.

Ghost investigations uncovered the story of a sergeant who shot himself in the guard house while handling his pistol. Some ghost hunters have spotted his ghost outside the building, appearing as a vertical blue mist or cloud. A compelling photograph of this ghost—who was seen after ghost hunters verbally invited him to appear—is posted on www.hollowhill.com. The photographer, Fiona Broome, named this ghost the man in blue.

Inside the building, park staff denied they had experienced ghostly activity. I, however, detected a dark male presence, brooding and angry. His anger was not directed at visitors, but at himself.

ANN STARRETT MANSION

74 Adams Street
Port Townsend 98368

A ghost roams this magnificent Victorian mansion. By all accounts, the spirit is feminine, and many are quick to believe it is the ghost of Ann Starrett. But a former employee of the bed-and-breakfast inn is certain the ghost is that of the Starrett family nanny, whose name is unknown. With no other identity than the nanny, the old woman has become a little intolerant of anyone who says anything uncomplimentary about the old house or the man who built it. Since the mansion has been called the crown jewel of Pacific Northwest inns and a four-story architectural extravaganza, such comments are rare. However, weary travelers who gripe a bit may feel the wraith of the nanny,

This spectacular mansion was built in 1899 by George E. Starrett at a cost of six thousand dollars. For this wealthy contractor, the project was a labor of love. Every aspect of the mansion was designed to please Ann Starrett and reflect her beauty. Two architectural features stand out and have attracted the attention of the Smithsonian Institution as well as members of the European architectural community.

The octagon that caps the tower over the entry was created by a New York artist George Chapman at the request of George Starrett. The dome of the octagon is a solar calendar on which Ann Starrett's likeness was used in renderings of the four seasons and the four virtues. On the first day of winter, fall, summer, and spring, sunshine hits the ruby-tinged glass and casts a red light onto the panel depicting the new season.

Rising into the domed tower, the other architectural feature continues to amaze builders and architects. The story told is that George Starrett met a man on the streets of Port Townsend one day who had some intriguing ideas about construction techniques. Starrett invited the man to his office and asked him to come up with a unique staircase that would rise to the fourth floor of his home. The strange builder agreed and then shut off part of the mansion, concealing his work until the day he finished. When the shrouds came down, Starrett stood in awe of a cantilevered staircase that rose to the fourth floor without central support. The structure is so mystifying that the Smithsonian Institution has offered to dismantle the staircase to determine how it was built and what features have enabled it to stand for more than one hundred years.

With all this love and attention to detail, it is reasonable to suspect that the spirits of George and Ann Starrett still haunt their fabulous mansion. They may be about somewhere in the huge mansion, but a former innkeeper told me that the most active ghost in the house in that of the nanny. The Starretts had only one child, Edwin Morris Starrett (1894-1981), but they employed a full-time nanny to watch over their active child. The nanny's private room on the second floor was furnished with a mirrored armoire. Guests and house staff have seen the partial image of an austere woman in that mirror. Those visiting the mansion who have complained a bit about Port Townsend weather, the tedious ferry crossing of Puget Sound, or a long drive have felt a tap on the head reminding them that complainers aren't tolerated in this beautiful, happy home.

The nanny also turns lights on and off, causes pictures to fall from the walls, and generates an atmosphere of displeasure if the guests who occupy her room don't keep it neat and tidy. Staff members working late in the evening have noticed the shadow of a woman in a Victorian gown moving up the stairs, never down. Also, in the grand parlor the tingling of fine crystal has been heard by the inn's guests as they sit admiring the antiques and view of the town

In the fall of 2005, the Ann Starrett Mansion was closed and up for sale. It has since re-opened and attracts admirers from all over the Pacific Northwest who can appreciate the history of this historic mansion.

THE BELMONT RESTAURANT, SALOON & HOTEL

Sterming Block
925 Water Street
Port Townsend 98368
360-385-3007

The old man shuffles about the place, oblivious to visitors, staff, and furnishings that have been relocated over the years. As the old man moves, the worn, salt-marked seaman's cap on his head seems to float on his thick, white, curly hair. A white mustache and beard fill half his face, leaving the other half—including his eyes—dark and indistinct. A dark sweater rises over his neck only to be concealed by a frayed pea coat similar to those worn by early-twentieth-century merchant seamen. The lightness of his hair and beard and darkness of his clothing sometimes blend together, giving the impression that the entire image is gray. When the light is bright or his energy low, the image is pale and fully transparent because this man, seen crossing the lobby or sitting on the stairs, is a ghost.

The old sailor, seen by visitors to the historic Belmont Restaurant, Saloon & Hotel, may not be alone. Many suspect that several ghosts haunt this establishment. With such a colorful history, it would be odd if only one ghost haunted the old sailor's saloon.

The Belmont Saloon opened its doors in 1885. Constructed by George Sterming, the shrewd entrepreneur, it catered to sailors and travelers who had few choices for food, lodging, or entertainment on the waterfront of old Port Townsend. The pier behind the establishment was the western terminus of the Seattle ferry and only a short distance from docks, piers, and warehouses devoted to fishing, timber transport, and other commercial enterprises. Within days of opening the Belmont, George Sterming was on his way to becoming a wealthy man. He served strong whiskey and hardy food and provided a convivial atmosphere for common seamen, ship's officers, cargo brokers, merchants, bankers, gamblers, hustlers, and prostitutes.

Wild banter, pandemonium, and confusion filled the place, laced with the pungent odor of cigar smoke. Deals were made, business plans were hatched, and the unwary were relieved of their cash. The mayhem was made even greater as panic-stricken passengers disembarked from the ferry after a storm-tossed crossing of Puget Sound only to find themselves in a saloon that seemed to be the very gates of hell.

All this created strong environmental imprints that sensitive visitors can detect. The cacophony of the past's mob of drinkers and gamblers sometimes breaks the silence of the modern, charming Belmont Hotel lobby. Apparitions of an old sailor, a woman with a feathered hat, and a bartender with a long handle-bar mustache startle guests. More often, the lobby feels as though it were filled with unseen people, creating a crowded sensation. Some of these ghosts create cold spots or leave their marks on film or digital images. Some ghost hunters suspect that the ghost of George Sterming is there, too. The doorway between the street and the lobby is a good place to hunt for these spirits. In the old days, a steady flow of customers kept the doors swinging.

Today, the Belmont Hotel offers four rooms on the second floor. In the nineteenth century, as many as ten sailors might have slept in one of these rooms. On the main floor, a fine restaurant serves up regional favorites that are a far cry from the crude fare devoured by the hungry, drunk clientele of the old Belmont Saloon.

OSCAR'S GHOST

The Inn at Port Hadlock
310 Hadlock Bay Road
Port Hadlock 98339
360-385-7030
www.innatporthadlock.com

Locals in this small but busy Puget Sound community often tell inquisitive visitors about an alcohol factory that was turned into a hotel and a rambunctious ghost that still haunts the premises. Depending on the storyteller, it can sound like a far-fetched legend or an intriguing story. The idea that a 1940s industrial building could become a stylish hotel sounds unlikely and arouses suspicions that a fun-loving local is spinning a yarn. But a short drive on Hadlock Bay Road past the main intersection of town takes visitors around a small bay to the portico of the impressive Inn at Port Hadlock.

The massive concrete beams of the former industrial structure blend with the stylish renovations of a modern inn, and even without entering the building, it is clear that the stories have at least one element of truth. Inside the manager's office, several photographs show gritty industrial scenes affirming that the place was, for several decades, an alcohol factory. The spacious lobby once housed the boilers. If you wander around the second-floor suites, you can see the massive concrete beams that supported vats filled with thousands of gallons of wood alcohol. Some of the hotel staff can tell you the history of the factory.

In the 1930s, when timber and fishing were the top industries on Puget Sound, a few enterprising fellows realized that huge piles of scrap wood and sawdust could be used to produce wood alcohol. They built a factory on the edge of a small bay to secure water transport for the incoming wood and outgoing tanks of alcohol. At its height during World War II, the factory was operated around the clock with a small skeleton crew working the graveyard shift.

Late one night, a worker named Oscar walked across the opening of a huge vat, balancing on a long, narrow beam. This was the way workers moved across the collection of vats, checking temperatures and removing floating debris. Oscar may have been overcome by the fumes or he might have been sipping a bit of the product mixed with molasses, a custom of the graveyard-shift workers. In any case, he lost his balance, fell into a vat of alcohol, and drowned. His nearly pickled body was found by the day shift.

Oscar was buried in a nearby cemetery, but that doesn't stop him from going to work each night. So many people have reported the partial apparition of a grimy, bearded fellow in coveralls, smelling of raw alcohol. Locals are certain the ghost is Oscar. Late in the evening, the pungent odor of alcohol can be detected in the second-floor hallway. It is strongest near the lobby. Moving like an invisible cloud, the odor has been detected passing from one end of the hall to the other, then back again. Oscar still makes his rounds from vat to vat.

By all accounts, Oscar is quiet and does not disturb guests. A former staff member described him as a short, slim fellow with a black, stubby beard. He wears a grimy cap and dirty gray coveralls that were probably white when new.

In the lobby of the Inn at Port Hadlock, sensitive visitors detect the clanking of heavy machinery, the rumble of the boilers that once filled the large space, and the presence of unseen workers. As a tribute to the history of the place, massive steel bolts and rings can be found on the walls. The best time to experience the auditory remnants of the alcohol factory is late in the evening when the lobby is darkened and the inn's guests are in bed or in the popular bar that provides a view of the marina and Indian Island.

NEGATIVE ENERGY AT THE GRANGE

Gig Harbor Grange
445 Wollochet Drive Northwest
Gig Harbor 98335
253-858-9986

The Gig Harbor Grange is the kind of place that inspires teenagers to park there at night. Concealed by the trees, people tell stories about creepy shadows and unseen forces that bump their cars, damping their passion. Other visitors to the site, by day or night, have posted reports of a strange energy, unexplained lights, strong blasts of wind on calm days, and other bizarre experiences that have been interpreted as para-normal. Most of these reports lack compelling evidence.

Drop-off recycling bins located on the property are reportedly neat and tidy at night, only to be found scattered in the morning. Some locals believe a deceased Grange member is unhappy with the bins and wants them off the property. But no one has captured photographic, video, or audio evidence of paranormal phenomena. It is more likely that homeless people in the area visit the bins at night to hunt for useful items. They scatter the contents to make the search a quick one and leave without cleaning up.

With this kind of information posted on the Web and in other publications, suspicion does not run high that the Gig Harbor Grange is, indeed, a site where paranormal phenomena may be experienced. My visit, however, led to a fascinating impression.

Late one morning in mid-November 2005, under overcast skies, the Grange parking lot sat deserted. Traffic on Wollochet Drive was light, and few cars came to a stop in front of the building on Artondale Drive. After walking the grounds for a few minutes, the atmosphere changed. The breezy air became still, heavy, and oppressive. These impressions were strongest in the center of the parking lot. While walking several times through this area, I found the strongest spot about twenty-five feet from the Grange building on a line extending westward from the north wall. The spot was about ten feet across and somewhat circular. Within the circle was a strong impression of negative energy. I experienced an intense feeling of being pulled downward into the ground, a loss of strength and energy, and a creepy feeling that someone angry was doing the pulling.

Looking at Google Earth maps and images of the site, I noted that the Grange building sits at the head of a narrow waterway called Wollochet Bay. Locations such as this were favored by Indian tribes as sites for permanent villages or temporary camp sites while hunting and fishing. Also, it is possible that this site was used for burials, or maybe warring tribes fought here. In any case, some restless spirit or intense environmental imprint of the hatred, fear, or revenge harbored by Indians may be responsible for the negative energy at the Grange.

USS *TURNER JOY* (DD-951)

300 Washington Avenue
Bremerton 98337-5668
360-792-2457
www.hnsa.org/ships/turnerjoy.htm

It has been said that every ship is haunted. Whether the vessel is a historic windjammer or a late-twentieth-century steel ship, there is something about long cruises, lonely vigils thousands of miles from home, or sailing into harm's way that creates strong emotional imprints. In the case of warships, sailors who die on board may remain trapped or choose to stay with their shipmates.

The USS *Turner Joy* stands a final, lonely watch at a pier in Bremerton, with a lively crew of maritime-history buffs and sailors who could not leave a proud warship untended. But it also has a few ghosts creeping around its decks.

The Vietnam-era USS Turner Joy, *berthed in Bremerton, still has a ghost crew aboard.*

Launched in Seattle in 1959 and named for Admiral Charles Turner Joy (1895-1956), the destroyer earned fame when it and the destroyer *Maddox* came under fire by North Vietnamese torpedo boats on August 4, 1964. This brief combat, which came to be known as the Gulf of Tonkin Incident, was a key element in the U.S. decision to embark on a military campaign in southeast Asia that was to be long and exceedingly painful. The *Turner Joy* was deployed with the Seventh Fleet through 1973. It participated in several other naval deployments and exercises in the Arabian Sea until its retirement in 1990. During combat duty in October 1965, it suffered its most tragic event. A shell detonated in one of its five-inch gun mounts, killing three crew members. As with any warship, several accidents and cases of severe illness occurred on board, some of which ended with the deaths of young sailors and officers.

Today, the USS *Turner Joy* is a popular tourist destination and a good place to conduct a ghost hunt. At several locations below deck, the unseen presence of dead crew members has been detected. Cold spots are often discovered in both the aft gun turret and the engine room. On the bridge, sensitive visitors have detected the remnant sounds of a crew as they maneuver the ship in combat.

All moored vessels—especially steel ships—create odd sounds that are transmitted through the hull. These sounds may be mistaken for paranormal phenomena. A small audio recorder, carried while touring the ship, may enable the ghost hunter to sort through the array of noises, like passing vessels, waves lapping against the hull, or the chaffing of mooring cables. It is a good idea to find a spot near bulkhead doors and let a recorder run. The sound of a slamming hatch secured with chains to the bulkhead might be captured on tape.

BREMERTON COMMUNITY THEATRE

599 Lebo Boulevard
Bremerton 98310
360-373-5152
www.bremertoncommunitytheatre.org

Theaters, large and small, are places where dreams are played out, where the most delicate emotions are put on display, and where exaltation, disappointment, anxiety, and even fear are often mixed together in a single act or a stirring moment on stage. Theaters absorb these emotions and the essence of the countless gut-wrenching moments that make them part of the environment.

It isn't any wonder that sensitive people, and even those who don't feel very sensitive, detect these environmental imprints in theaters. Ghosts often inhabit theaters because actors, directors, dancers, musicians, and other creative people were so attached to the stage while they were alive that they can not leave a cherished place of a theatrical triumph or give up the possibility of a starring role yet to come. Adding to the mix are the spirits of those who sat in the audience and fell in love with a leading actor or actress or jealous stage hands who had the hots for cast members.

The little Bremerton Community Theatre is believed to have strong environmental imprints and a ghost or two. The present building, constructed in 1976, overlooks a narrow arm of Puget Sound and accommodates patrons with a large parking lot. The exterior has an industrial look, but the interior has all the charm of a cozy community theater. The company it houses was started during World War II to offer shipyard workers a little diversion from their wartime labor. The first drama director was Eddie Hammond, wife of prominent citizen Harry Hammond. Eddie Hammond is credited with establishing a tradition for widespread community involvement and support. The town's patronage has enabled the theater company to flourish for more than sixty years.

Hammond's love for this theater may have been so strong that she may be on the scene still, directing actors and monitoring backstage activity. Disembodied footsteps—those of a light-weight person wearing heels—have often been heard crossing the stage. There are occasional sightings of pale or transparent beings dancing or flying across the stage without visible legs. Sometimes props and articles of clothing fly onto the stage as if thrown by invisible hands from the wings. One report described a man in a tall hat, à la Dr. Seuss' cat, and a cape who appears on stage and in the back row of the theater.

Ghost hunters have detected an intense cold spot in a third-row seat, center, where a director might sit during rehearsals. In the catwalks above the stage, some people have spotted a dark, humanlike shape moving about. The area is always dimly lit, but the apparition does not have legs and its head is indistinct. Similar apparitions have been seen in the dressing rooms.

Other places to hunt for ghosts on the west side of Puget Sound:

The Palace Hotel

1004 Water Street
Port Townsend 98368
360-385-0773

Visitors and guests have encountered spirits dressed in Victorian gowns who appear lifelike. Also, people feel invisible hands brush past them as they walk the hallways. Orbs have been captured on film and in digital images at several places in the hotel.

The Rothschild House

418 Taylor Street
Port Townsend
360-385-1003

Built in 1868, the Rothschild House is now managed by the Jefferson County Historical Society. Paranormal reports include the sound of slamming doors and bizarre temperature fluctuations.

James and Hastings Building

900 Water Street
Port Townsend

Built in 1889, the ground floor of this large mercantile and residential building houses unique retail shops. A ghost that plays tricks was discovered there in 2003. He moves merchandise around, opens windows, and seems interested in female patrons of the shops.

Captain John Quincy Adams House

1028 Tyler Street
Port Townsend

This 1887 mansion was for sale in the fall of 2005. However, the property, recently purchased, is now undergoing renovations. Visitors have detected the ghosts of children as they run through the halls and front parlor.

CHAPTER 3

Communities South of Seattle

Ghost hunters have some fascinating experiences in the South Puget Sound communities. Historic towns such as Georgetown and Steilacoom were home to some flamboyant and rambunctious characters whose spirits still haunt their favorite restaurants, brothels, and alleys. In Tacoma, sister city and rival to Seattle, the ghosts of Indians and politicians add to the intrigue of the city. Tacoma's Point Defiance Park has a quiet atmosphere, spooky shadows, and a haunted legacy that makes the short trip from Seattle worthwhile. While in this area, ghost hunters should visit the grounds of the insane asylum in Lakewood.

GHOSTS OF THE WAYWARD GIRLS

Martha Washington Park (former site of the Martha Washington School)
6612 Fifty-Seventh Avenue South
Seattle 98118

Martha Washington Park stands at the shores of Lake Washington, vacant and strangely quiet. There is no playground, tennis court, or any other site for recreation except the expansive lawn broken by stands of century-old trees. If you walk the ten acres, you discover remnants of paved roads that once served the estate and school. Walking by the lakeshore, a few scattered blocks of stone are all that remain of the seawall. At the north end of the area, stone steps lead up from the beach past a thick grove of trees. Nothing else remains of a once grand estate that was turned into a reform school for girls except the ghosts who cannot leave this strange place.

Judge Everett T. Smith (1862-1933) purchased the land from John Wilson in 1889 and constructed a huge mansion with a caretaker's cottage and greenhouse. In 1920, the Seattle School District purchased the property and opened the Martha Washington School for Girls, a residential facility that was widely known as a reform school for troubled youth. The mansion was expanded with classrooms and a dormitory that housed up to seventy girls. The school closed in 1971. Two years later, the buildings were demolished. I could not find an explanation for the complete demolition of the place in the public historical record.

Residents in the area tell the story of a janitor who went on a crazed killing spree in the late 1950s, taking the lives of several girls and two staff members. He threw some of the bodies into Lake Washington and dropped two others down the well. Ghost hunters who have visited this site have reported disembodied sobbing and the touch of an invisible hand on their shoulders.

Some visitors have experienced creepy feelings and odd temperature changes at several places on the ten-acre site. The former location of the caretaker's cottage—marked by the small stone staircase that leads up from the beach—is particularly creepy. I sensed the presence of three or four people performing some kind of work at the top of these stairs. I also heard the muted sound of digging tools and men groaning, as if they were lifting something heavy.

Residents in the area usually refuse to speak to ghost hunters about this place. There may be many reasons for this. Perhaps they wish to discourage the traffic on the small, residential streets. One friendly man, eager to talk about the place, said that you can often see strange lights moving through the park at night, as if several people were walking in line, each with a candle or flashlight.

A map of the estate and school can be found online by accessing the Seattle Park Department's Web site, www.seattle.gov/parks/history/, and clicking on the Sherwood History Files link. This map indicates the position of the dormitory, gymnasium, greenhouse, caretaker's cottage, and mansion. This information can make a ghost hunt more efficient and specific for the spirit you seek. You may want to leave an audio recorder running at a particular location while you walk the grounds.

GHOSTS OF THE HEART BRIDGE

Kubota Garden
9817 Fifty-Fifth Avenue
Seattle 98118
206-684-4584 or 206-725-6050
www.kubota.org

Kubota Garden may be one of the most beautiful places in Seattle. Established on five acres of swamp land in 1927 by Japanese emigrant Fujitaro Kubota, the horticultural paradise contains a magnificent collection of plants—trees, shrubs, and grasses—artfully placed around waterways and ponds and accented with bridges, rock

Ghost hunters feel the rush of spirits dashing across the Heart Bridge in beautiful Kubota Garden.

outcroppings, manicured pathways, and sculptures. The self-taught gardener purchased the land to fulfill his dream of creating a garden that would display the beauty of the Pacific Northwest in the Japanese style of harmony and grace. His initial plantings attracted so much attention that Kubota's landscape and gardening company became one of the most successful in the region. Kubota died in 1973, leaving his son Tom to watch over the garden that had become so famous. In 1987, the city of Seattle acquired the garden and fostered the formation of the Kubota Garden Foundation. Today, the five-acre garden and a seventeen-acre surround of open space are maintained by the city's Department of Parks and a dedicated corps of volunteers. It is open to the public free of charge.

A stroll through the various theme areas of the garden gives the impression that many spirits reside there, seeking beauty, peace, and harmony. The placid ponds, tiny streams, and melodious waterfalls make it easy to meditate and get in touch with the spirituality of the place. But one location in particular seems to be a gathering place or conduit for active or restless spirits attached to the gardens.

The Heart Bridge was constructed in the mid-1930s and is one of the oldest architectural features of the gardens. It crosses Mapes Creek as it widens to form a broad pond. The bridge is wide enough to allow passage of a car but is intended for foot traffic only. Painted red, the structure resembles traditional bridges found on Kubota's home island, Shikoku, Japan.

When walking over this bridge from west to east, sensitive visitors may feel the rush of unseen men running past them as if they are being chased. The sensation is not detected when walking east to west. One psychic described the men as short, dressed in black or dark Asian clothing, and wearing small cloth hats. These spirits are frightened, but they dash across the bridge in silence.

There is no historical record of a civil disturbance taking place in the Kubota Garden. But in the early days of World War II, Japanese living in this neighborhood—including the Kubota family—were rounded up by military police and loaded on trucks destined for internment camps in Idaho. The sadness and horror of that experience may have created an energy vortex isolated at Heart Bridge.

After the war, Kubota and his sons, Tak and Tom, rebuilt the garden that had been abandoned since March 1942, demonstrating their desire to create a place of peace and harmony for the people of Seattle.

KOREAN CENTRAL BAPTIST CHURCH

1201 South Bailey Street
Seattle 98108-2765
206-767-5500

This building was constructed in 1927 when Georgetown was little more than a rambling collection of widely spaced shacks. The Masons funded the construction and used the place as a meeting hall and church. Local legend says the Masons conducted secret ceremonies there that included animal sacrifices. The more bizarre tales mention human sacrifices as well, but this is far beyond the borders of credibility.

After the Masons moved to better facilities, the building sat vacant for a few years before various renters tried to establish businesses there. None of them lasted long. In the early 1980s, the Korean Central Baptist Church of Seattle moved in and opened a school, seminary, and church on the upper floors of the building. This organization has occupied the property for more than twenty years. In the spring of 2006, most of the ground floor of this building was once again vacant and falling into disrepair. The corner space, though, houses Hansen's Florist Shop.

People who have spent time in the building and locals in the neighborhood have spread the word that there is something strange about the place. They report hearing slamming doors, groans and moans, short screams, and other weird sounds. Even people passing by on the street who happen to look in the large windows to view the vacant first floor hear strange sounds and see inexplicable shadows moving about the place. Also, some reports include an apparition of a man who haunts the old church. There is no descriptive information available, such as clothing, race or stature, which might lead to identification of this spirit.

The psychic shop that used to be across the street has gone out of business. In its place is a tax consultant. You may learn more about the strange happenings at this place if you can track down longtime residents of this neighborhood or talk to people in Hansen's Florist Shop.

While many ghost hunters suspect the bizarre practices of the Masons led to the spooky ambience and ghostly experiences many have had at this location, an alternative explanation may be found in a tragic accident. If you look at a map of the area and match it up with an aerial view by using Google Earth, you see an interesting connection between nearby Boeing Field and the location of a fatal plane crash described later in this chapter. When an airplane plowed into the neighborhood, several people on the ground were killed and others were unaccounted for. It is possible that the building at 1201 South Bailey Street was damaged by flying debris from the crash and the fires that followed. Perhaps the ghost of a victim wanders the premises now.

C-46 AIRPLANE CRASH SITE

916 South Harney Street
Georgetown
Seattle 98108-2744

There is something strange about the neighborhood surrounding 916 South Harney Street in Georgetown. Nearly all the buildings house commercial activities, stand amid large parking lots, and give the impression that everything runs smoothly around here. But since the early 1950s, few people have been comfortable living at this location. The frightening things they saw and the bizarre sensations they experienced drove them away. Locals reported flashes of light, the smell of smoke and burning human flesh, the sight of burning aviation fuel, and the sound of loud crashes when the street was empty. Eventually, the shacks, houses, and old boarding houses were torn down, the street widened, and new businesses established. But paranormal phenomena continue to occur on this street.

Many believe these strange occurrences are the result of an airplane crash in July 1949. Retired General Duncan Miller, owner of the civilian aircraft, witnessed the crash from the end of Boeing Field. At the time, Miller had recently mustered out of the U.S. Army Air

Corps and had started a charter airline—Air Transport Associates—with contracts to provide cargo and passenger service to military units in the Pacific Northwest. I interviewed Miller in January 2005 and he gave this account of the crash:

"That morning, the C-46 [a twin-engine, "tail-dragger" aircraft] was prepped as usual and fueled by a gang from the field's fueling service. A small amount of cargo was loaded on board, and then twenty-eight passengers lined up for boarding. Two of the passengers were drunk, so I told them they could not board the plane. The ranking officer of the group stepped up and said that he would personally secure the two men in their seats and make certain they didn't interfere with operation of the aircraft. With this assurance, I allowed the drunken men to board the plane and informed the pilot, Wilbur Fitch, of the situation.

"The C-46 taxied out and made a normal takeoff. They were less than a hundred feet off the ground when the plane yawed left and the prop of the left engine seem to lose RPMs. It was clear to me that the left engine was losing power. Later, we found out that the fueling gang put the wrong fuel in the left tank.

"The pilot leveled off and started a slow left turn to try a landing. He might have made it, except he hit a power line or telephone line, and this took a few miles per hour off his air speed. Still, he continued the turn. Then, he hit another power line. That caused the left wing to dip more, added some more yaw, and stalled the plane. They hit hard but flat and took out seven or eight houses and a boarding house. Fuel and wreckage flew everywhere, causing quite a few fires in the neighborhood, but the fuselage was pretty much intact.

"Luckily, everyone on board got off the plane. But those drunken guys, they must have been dazed and confused or sobered up quick and thought their buddies were still inside the burning fuselage because they ran back in. We found them later, inside the plane, dead from the smoke and flames.

"I got to the scene within a minute or so of the impact and helped drag injured and dead people to a grove of trees. [That grove of trees still stands at the site along Carlton Avenue South.] Several people in the houses hit by the plane were killed. A lot of folks in the neighborhood were injured. Medics arrived from Boeing Field and set up a first-aid station in those trees. I know some of the people hit by the plane died at that aid station in those trees."

The official death toll listed five killed on the ground as well as two passengers. According to Miller's account, the two passengers might have survived had they not reentered the burning wreckage.

A photograph of the destruction published in Seattle newspapers reminded many of a World War II bombing raid. For days after the crash, people in the neighborhood relived the tragedy when they perceived the sound of the impact, an explosion, and the screams and cries of the wounded. Even today, sensitive ghost hunters may detect environmental imprints or hauntings of this event in the grove of trees, at the South Harney Street address, and at nearby sites in the neighborhood.

GHOST OF THE GIRL ON A SWING

Des Moines City Marina Park
22307 Dock Avenue
Des Moines 98198

Marina Park, with its beach, creek, and playground, sits at the north end of the city marina. A small playground is located at the south end of the marina. Ghost hunters should not be confused by signs that proclaim each site "Marina Park."

The ghost of a little girl named Diana is said to appear at Marina Park each year on January 8. This date most likely marks her death. Members of AGHOST and other ghost hunters, however, have detected spirits at this site on random dates. The ghost of Diana is often seen walking on the beach and swinging. I experienced this ghost on November 9, 2005, when I saw what appeared to be an empty swing—the one closest to the beach in the set of six swings—move forward and backward for more than five minutes while the remaining five swings sat motionless. Also, the seat of the moving swing was depressed, as if someone was sitting in it, while the seats of the others were more horizontal.

The beach park includes the waterfront area at the edge of Puget Sound, a large sandbox with the swings, a grassy field, and the creek.

A few buildings are scattered about for maintenance equipment and special events. The city of Des Moines, Washington, was founded at this site, but the first residential area was located inland. Several lumber mills were built along the creek. One of them burned in a massive fire in 1894. After the other mills were dismantled, a children's home was established on high ground above the creek. The children had access to the creek and beach, where they played ball games and had picnics. Later, cabins were added for weekend and summer visitors. It is likely that a few tragedies occurred there when the creek swelled with winter rains, flooding the area, or when young swimmers ventured too far offshore.

Diana died either in the creek or on the beach. The precise history is unknown. At least one psychic investigator believes Diana's death was accidental and that it occurred on January 8 of an unspecified year. The psychic sensed that the playground was the little girl's favorite place. She spent hours there, often alone, daydreaming and contemplating her future.

AGHOST investigators have detected the presence of several young spirits, as well as the spirit of an old man who might have been the groundskeeper. In one of the maintenance buildings, one ghost hunter discovered an entity who wanted investigators to leave the park.

GHOST OF THE CHILD CYCLIST

Narrows Viewpoint on Five Mile Drive
Point Defiance Park
5400 North Ruston Way
Tacoma 98407-3224
253-305-1000

Point Defiance is a paradise. Heavily wooded with natural vegetation, it gives visitors a clear idea of the region's condition before adventurers and settlers arrived. Lush fern grottoes, stands of redwoods, and carpets of natural grasses create such a serene atmosphere that it is hard to believe that a brutal murder occurred there.

While driving or cycling the five-mile road that winds through the Tacoma peninsula, shafts of sunlight penetrate the thick stands of trees.

Odd shadows give a sense that apparitions of Indians or buckskin-clad explorers might cross the path at any turn. But a different apparition has been spotted there that has left witnesses shaken and screaming.

In 1988, a little girl named Carol was riding her bike through the vast park. Rounding a turn near the Tacoma Narrows Viewpoint—a point of interest that offers a great view—someone took advantage of the fact that little Carol was alone. The attacker jumped from the brush, pulled her from her bike, and brutally murdered her, leaving her body at the edge of the water. A search party found the little girl, but her murderer was never apprehended. In fact, there were virtually no clues at the crime scene, and the police investigation yielded nothing. Many believe, however, that the murderer was a local person who frequently returns to the scene of the crime.

People passing by the Narrows Viewpoint report the sound of a child's bicycle bell, ringing several times, yet no child cyclist appears on the single-lane paved road. Others have actually seen the apparition of the little victim. She stands at the edge of the road next to her bike, as if awaiting help. At times, the apparition looks so lifelike that drivers have gotten out of their cars and approached Carol, asking if she needed help. One witness, who got within a few feet of the ghost, reported that she had no eyes.

Perhaps Carol's ghost cannot find her way out of the wooded peninsula. The road, cloaked in shadows and surrounded by tall trees, may confuse her. Carol may not know what direction to ride home. Ghost hunters investigating this location should attempt to record EVP. Carol may ask for help from anyone who shows interest in her. Female ghost hunters have more luck with this ghost, leading to speculation that Carol's murderer was a male.

THE PAGODA ON FIVE MILE DRIVE

Point Defiance Park
5400 North Ruston Way
Tacoma 98407-3224
253-305-1000

More than a century ago, the Pagoda was a trolley-car station marking the end of the line. For some passengers, it also marked the end of their lives. At least three ghosts roam this Japanese-inspired building that now serves as a reception hall, wedding venue, and tourist attraction on Point Defiance.

The large building sits on land that slopes away from the parking area. Visitors enter on the second floor and descend the stairs to the first floor, which opens onto a large patio protected from the breezes off Puget Sound by the high peaked roof and surrounding trees. Originally constructed as a rustic shelter for visitors from the nearby city of Tacoma, the place was a recreation spot with picnic areas and boating facilities. In 1914, the elaborate Pagoda was built on the site to serve as a social center for important events, catering more to Tacoma's upper classes than its common citizens, who frequented the place for a day's respite from the city. A small aid station was established on the first floor and a portion of the second floor continued to serve as a trolley station until after World War II.

The facility's staff members as well as visitors have reported hearing disembodied footsteps move down the stairs on the building's east side. The sound is loud and sharp, as if the ghost is wearing hard-soled shoes or boots. Some witnesses have also reported cold spots on the stairs as the auditory phenomenon passed them. The sound seems to disappear when the unseen spirit reaches the bottom of the stairs. Visitors have also heard coughing, sighing, brief shouts, and the sound of wet clothing or towels hitting the floor at various places on the lower level.

Some of this ghostly activity may be attributable to a man who killed himself in the restroom on the lower level in the early 1920s. The legend says that the man and his wife, newlyweds, took the trolley car each Saturday, traveling from town to the Point Defiance ferry landing. There, the wife boarded a small boat, with a few other passengers, and crossed to Vashon Island to visit her parents. The husband spent the day relaxing on the beach or in the gardens. Late in the afternoon, the wife would return from Vashon Island and the two would take the trolley car home. One day, this pleasant habit led to disaster.

As the flotilla of small boats approached the dock, rough water and strong winds caused the wife's boat to take on water. The vessel quickly became unbalanced and capsized. The crowd at the dock, including the young husband, was horrified to see their loved ones dumped into the frigid water. Legend says that the husband had the presence of mind to pull a small spyglass from his pocket. He used the glass to watch his young wife drown. Having such an up close and personal

The Pagoda, once an elaborate bath house and social center, stands in Tacoma's Point Defiance Park. At least three ghosts are said to haunt the building.

view of the tragedy, he walked, stunned, to the Pagoda, descended the stairs to the lower-floor restroom and shot himself. His ghost is said to haunt the building, creating the disembodied footsteps heard on the staircase.

The pale, partial apparition of a woman dressed in white also appears at the Pagoda. She has been spotted on the lower level and in the main entry at the second floor. This ghost may be searching for her suicidal husband.

A third ghost haunts the patio off the lower floor. It is believed to be the spirit of a homeless man who died slumped against the exterior wall of the building in the early 1990s. He is an older man with a short beard, black sailor's cap, and heavy boots. When approached, he looks up from where he died and then vanishes.

POLITICAL GHOSTS

Old Tacoma City Hall
South Seventh Street at Pacific Avenue
Tacoma 98402-2202

There is something about old civic buildings that traps or attracts ghosts. No matter what city you visit, if you are looking for ghosts, find the nearest historic courthouse, city hall, state capitol, or legislative house. Delve into the history and you will find a ghost story that has some credibility. The old Tacoma City Hall is a good place to start.

The Italian Renaissance building was constructed in 1893 as a monument to the pride of the city and as a magnet for developers and investors. The building opened on the eve of a nationwide economic crash. Still, Tacoma's mayor and city council settled in nicely and weathered the hard times. The building's fancy brickwork, terra-cotta ornamentation, and huge clock tower served as the hub of Tacoma's social, political, and economic growth. A lot of politicians came and went, fighting for causes, taking bribes, and stabbing their proverbial political foes in the back. Particularly throughout the 1920s and 1930s, public funds supported a lot of schemes while other deals failed to make the right connections. With that kind of business going on, the passionate people became disillusioned or so caught up in their causes that they couldn't leave city hall, even when they died.

In 1959, Tacoma's city offices were relocated to a modern building, but the spirits of politicians and crusaders stayed behind. Their activity increased in 1970 when the building was renovated and again in 1980 when additional modifications were made to turn the place into professional offices.

Ghosts of Tacoma's early politicians are still making deals in the 1893 City Hall.

Security staff, tenants, and visitors have reported an elevator that goes up and down without activation of the call buttons. Some visitors have heard doors slam by unseen hands. Sometimes locks are set, locking people out of their offices. On every floor, lights turn on and off. When tenants leave for the night, security staff members have assured that all lights are off. But in the middle of the night, all lights on an entire floor mysteriously turn on. At times the spooky activity and eerie atmosphere have been so extreme that several guards have quit.

If you walk the old halls when the building is quiet, you can hear the rush of busy, invisible people passing by. You may also hear a disembodied cough or someone nervously clearing his throat, perhaps before appearing before the city council.

GHOST OF THE CONSTANT USHER

Pantages (Roxy) Theatre
901 Broadway
Tacoma 98402
253-591-5894

On January 7, 1918, famed vaudeville producer and impresario Alexander Pantages (1876-1936) opened this magnificent theater. Known for the Hollywood theater that bares his name, Pantages had a broad and enlightened view of the entertainment needs of the country during the waning years of World War I. He knew that vaudeville—live stage performance by singers, dancers, and comedians—would remain the number one line of entertainment for the masses while silent movies were just getting started. Being a native of Seattle, Alexander Pantages included his hometown in the vaudeville circuit, which ranged from cities along the Mississippi River to the West Coast. The theater he built in Tacoma was designed by architect B. Marcus Priteca and included a lavish interior with a huge skylight and white granite exterior that made the place look more like a grand hotel than a music hall.

Like ships, most theaters are thought to be haunted. Ghosts found in these old theaters include dedicated directors, talented musicians, ardent fans who never missed a performance, unfortunate stagehands who were killed in freak accidents with rigging or electrical equipment, and actors who were so addicted to applause from an adoring audience that they could never leave the stage. Historic theaters in Los Angeles, San Francisco, New Orleans, New York, and Chicago have ghosts such as these. But the Pantages Theatre in Seattle also has the ghost of a dedicated employee who is always close at hand in the darkness to help patrons to their seats.

Patrons who arrive late for a performance at this revitalized theater may be assisted to their reserved seats by an unseen presence. An intense cold spot brings them to a stop at the very row where they are to be seated. Some patrons even feel the disembodied hand of the ghost usher as he touches their elbows or shoulders. Some theatergoers have actually seen this ghost. He appears in the darkness as a short, stocky man without distinct facial features, wearing a dark jacket and pants. His face also appears dark. Whew patrons turn to thank the usher for his help findings their seats, they find that he has vanished.

HAUNTS OF TB PATIENTS

Emerald Queen Casino Hotel
5700 Pacific Highway East
Fife 98424
253-922-2000
www.emeraldqueen.com/hotel.html

This pleasant hotel and casino stands on the site of an old building that was once a hospital. If you view the site using satellite images such as Google Earth, you will notice that this prime property is sparsely developed except for the casino. A lot of open space surrounding a building can sometimes mean that the land is inhospitable. A little research may reveal local legends and ghost stories that disturb people in the area and deter builders and developers from using the land.

For decades, the hospital that sat on the land served people who had tuberculosis. So many patients died there that a crematorium was installed in the basement for the disposal of infected corpses. This history gave rise to the urban legend that the ghosts of TB victims wander the facility and surrounding open spaces looking for their bodies.

After the hospital closed, the building became administrative headquarters for the Puyallup Tribe. Placing the tribe's offices there had something to do with the location of an ancient village near the shore of the Puyallup River. Some locals say the land is sacred to the Indians and was the site of burials. If ghost activity or spirit unrest occurred there, the Indians aren't talking.

A few years ago, the five-story structure that served as tribal offices and a hospital was torn down. The four-story Emerald Queen Casino Hotel replaced the former building and offers just about everything you could find in Vegas, including ghosts. The top floor of the hotel seems to be the most active. A woman's cries, children's sobbing, and men's moaning can be heard. These paranormal phenomena used to be encountered on the fifth floor of the tribe's headquarters. It seems that the ghosts have descended one floor and have found new rooms and hallways to haunt.

Objects placed on tables in guest rooms disappear then reappear. Lights turn off and on. Television remotes are activated by unseen hands. Elevators are often called to the fifth floor by invisible beings. Ghostly activity also occurs in the basement—generally off-limits to guests—in spaces formerly occupied by the crematorium.

The hotel accommodates people who only want to roam around the top floor looking for ghosts, but ghost hunters must stop at the front desk, identify themselves, and explain the purpose of their visit. The best way to experience the strange phenomena is to spend a night on the haunted fourth floor. It is interesting to note that, although this floor is spiritually active, the old hospital had fewer than five floors. This is an intriguing mystery for some eager ghost hunters.

GHOSTS IN THE LONG BOATS

Gog-le-hi-ti Wetlands
North Levee Road West of Fifty-Fourth Avenue East (past Frank Albert Road East)
Tacoma 98404-4974

Looking outward from high ground to the dark waters of the Puyallup River, it is easy to imagine a bark canoe gliding over the water, paddled by Indians, laden with fish and ducks. At this particular location, you may not have to use your imagination to see such things. This stretch of the river, known as the Gog-le-hi-ti Wetlands, was once a hunting area used by the Puyallup Indians. They used bark canoes to glide through the grasses and thickets at the water's edge, snaring birds and ducks, shooting geese with bow and arrow, and fishing with spears. It is reported that burials took place there, too.

Many visitors to the area have reported ghostly canoes that glide a short distance toward shore and then disappear before touching the land. These apparitions appear for only a few seconds and without sound. The number of Indians seen in the canoe varies from one to as many as three. They appear not to notice their spectators even when they are only a few feet away from the astonished bird watchers, fishermen, or ghost hunters who frequent the area.

Ghost hunters have also reported the apparition of an old man and his dog. They walk the edge of North Levee Road, on the river side and appear lifelike. People driving the road notice the pair through their windshields, but after passing, the man and his dog are not seen in the rear-view mirrors.

Before traveling to this site, ghost hunters should review satellite-image service, such as Google Earth, to view the open space and get oriented. Be cautious if you stand on the banks of the river. Some of them are steep and unstable.

BAIR DRUG AND HARDWARE STORE

1617 Lafayette Street
Steilacoom 98388
253-588-9668

By all accounts, W. L. Bair was a stickler for details. The day he opened his pharmacy in 1895 he checked the inventory twice and made certain the cash-drawer contents matched the ledger in the back office. Known as Cub to his friends, the meticulous pharmacist offered the good people of Steilacoom everything a modern pharmacy should offer, plus a hardware supply, a handsome soda fountain, and a pot-belly stove. Cub kept the fire in the store stoked to provide

The ghost of pharmacist Cub Bair is still trying to run this historic shop.

a warm and welcoming atmosphere for customers and the retired men who spent hours each day in the pharmacy playing checkers. When Cub died, he didn't let death stand in the way of putting in a full day's work in his beloved pharmacy.

Something about being a ghost, though, got in the way of doing things to perfection. When the pharmacy became a café, Cub tried his hand at toasting bagels and operating electric kitchen appliances and the soda fountain. The many stories about bizarre phenomena that occurred in the building suggest Cub had lost his touch. Bagels mysteriously burned, appliances malfunctioned, and a lot of other weird things happened. One employee witnessed several bottles of a new sauce fly off the shelf. The bottles didn't fall to the floor, store manager Rosa Kreger reported. They flew across the room. Others saw coffee pots spin, doors swing open, and lights sway.

Cub Bair seems happy with the way his store was converted to a café and museum. It may be all the antiques that have caused the ghost to mellow. Old medicine bottles, small hardware items, and a bank of postal boxes at the rear of the building probably make him feel as though the clock has been turned back to 1895.

For quite a long time, things were so quiet in the building that people suspected Cub had moved on, in a spiritual sense. In the fall of 2005, though, a ghost hunter detected a spirit presence in the drug store next to the wall of postal boxes. While seated at the small table located there, several patrons have heard humming and other curious vocalizations that seem to come from an unseen being standing close behind them. They have also reported the sound of breathing, with a little wheezing.

Some people suggest that Cub Bair also haunts the bank next door. Ghost hunters who seek this entity should investigate buildings and open spaces at the intersection of Lafayette and Wilkes.

E. R. ROGERS RESTAURANT

1702 Commercial Street
Steilacoom 98388
253-582-0280

At first view, Catherine was enamored by the young and dashing Captain Edwin R. Rogers as he brought his ship to an anchorage and stepped ashore in Steilacoom in 1852. Word quickly spread that the captain, a wealthy merchant and owner of the schooner he commanded, was headed north in search of gold. But on seeing the beautiful country surrounding Puget Sound and the quaint town that lay before him, he decided to relocate his shipping business to the tiny port and settle down. The beautiful Catherine may have played a role in that decision because after a few months, she and Edwin were married.

Many years later in 1891, the couple built their dream home, a 4,582-square-foot mansion that now stands across the street from the captain's first anchorage. But the couple, and their large family, had little time to enjoy the seventeen-room house and its magnificent views. The captain's investments were hit hard in the nationwide economic crash of 1893, and he lost much of his wealth. Sadly, the Rogers family moved out, but years later, Catherine returned to the house she loved so much. She may have been jealous of Hattie Bair, wife of drugstore owner Cub Bair, who bought the place in

1920 and turned it into a rooming house. Maybe she was curious about the fine restaurant that served patrons amid the Victorian elegance she knew so well. Maybe she was so attached to the mansion that she simply could not bare to reside anywhere else. Whatever her reason, there is little doubt that Catherine Rogers has returned home to her mansion by the shore, undeterred by her death.

People who work in the E. R. Rogers Restaurant can tell you some fascinating stories about the ghostly activities that take place there. Lights have flashed on just after the last person has locked the doors and left. Alarms have been triggered in the middle of the night, calling police to the house. They enter with drawn guns, expecting to find a burglar, but the place is empty. When a police dog is brought to the scene, the well-trained animal refuses to enter the house.

Catherine's ghost also tinkers with electrical wiring, electronic equipment such as VCRs and DVD players, and small appliances at the bar and in the kitchen. The ghost has also unnerved workers

The ghosts of two strong-willed women roam the E. R. Rogers Restaurant, formerly a mansion, trying to capture the attention of visitors.

brought in for special jobs. A crew of carpet cleaners went into the building after hours to work. After cleaning one carpet, they left and refused to reenter the building. Something spooky about Catherine's presence drove them away.

Restaurant patrons have witnessed ghostly activity, too. One man, sitting in the upstairs bar, saw a woman's stocking-clad legs appear at his eye level. Others have seen candles and glasses fly off tables. Depressions appear in the carpet as if an unseen person were walking on it, and partial apparitions appear in mirrors and windows of a woman with an elegant hairdo in a Victorian dress.

There has been no confirmation that the ghost of the E. R. Rogers Restaurant is, indeed, that of Catherine Rogers. Some ghost hunters wonder if the female spirit is that of Hattie Bair, who operated a rooming house in the building from 1920 to 1940. Some say that the female spirit haunts the place because she killed herself in an upstairs room. If Hattie and Catherine's deaths can be discovered through historical research and one is found to have been a suicide, we may better understand this ghost and know for certain who haunts the restaurant.

GHOST OF THE HANGED MAN

Starling Street northeast of Puyallup Street
Steilacoom 98388
253-584-4133 (Steilacoom Historical Association)

In the early morning and again at dusk, a strange-looking man walks Starling Street near Puyallup Street. Sometimes he wanders as far as Pacific Avenue, but he usually stays at the northeast end of the street where the jail used to stand. The man's head is cocked at a peculiar angle, and if you get a close look at him, you will see that a hangman's noose rests about his neck. Ghost hunters who have seen this ghost from a short distance say that the noose is bloodied and the man's eyes look as though they may pop from their sockets. The reason this fellow looks so strange is that he was hanged in 1888. His body was placed in a pauper's grave, but his ghost walks the streets of Steilacoom looking for his cow and, perhaps, the man he murdered.

The story goes that Joshua M. Bates was a poor man with only one possession of any value. That possession was a cow that was well known around town because she wandered freely, grazing on grasses that grew in vacant lots and open pastures. Bates sold the milk she gave, and the few cents it brought each day kept him alive.

One day, Bates could not find his cow. When he asked a stranger if he had seen the animal, the man gave Bates a false lead, suggesting Andrew Byrd had taken her. In a rage, Bates searched the saloons along Main Street and found Byrd. A wild confrontation followed as Bates accused him of stealing her and Byrd denied knowing where the cow was. It ended when Bates drew a pistol and shot Byrd.

The story goes that, with his dying breath, Byrd asked the gathering crowd to let Bates go without punishment. The poor man had lost his temper and let his simple mind be ruled by frantic emotions. The crowd heard Byrd's last words, but moments after Byrd died, Bates was arrested. After a few drinks to the memory of a good and popular man, Byrd's friends became a mob of vigilantes. They marched to the Starling Street jail, tore open the cell, and dragged the murderer to a tree at the edge of town. They fashioned a hangman's noose, and in minutes, Joshua Bates swung from a branch.

The next day, the dark atmosphere that hung over Steilacoom was made worse when someone found Bates' cow wandering near the railroad tracks. Ghost hunters have never encountered the ghost of Andrew Byrd on Main Street or anywhere else in town. But Joshua Bates' spirit still walks the streets looking for that cow and the man he killed. He might also be on the lookout for the vigilantes who hung him.

If you visit the charming town of Steilacoom in search of Andrew Byrd, Joshua Bates, or the elusive Bates cow, check out the train tracks next to the ferryboat pier. Bates' cow might have been found at this spot. Also, ghost hunters report the disembodied scream of someone who, decades ago, was struck by a train there.

GHOST OF THE DROWNED WOMAN OF WAUGHOP LAKE

Campus of Pierce College
9401 Farwest Drive Southwest at Steilacoom Boulevard
Lakewood 98498-7213
253-964-6500 (Campus Visitor's Information)

Some ghost hunters have published Internet reports of ghost activity at this location and called the body of water Pierce Lake. This is an error arising from the fact that Pierce College stands next to the lake. The lake is named after Dr. John W. Waughop, superintendent of the nearby Western State Asylum from 1880 to 1897.

To visit the lake, drive to the rear of the campus and park behind the Dental Hygiene Building in the visitor spaces. The lake can be viewed from the parking lot. Two pathways lead to the walking trail that surrounds the lake.

There are many reports of a bizarre woman's voice heard in the morning hours when the wind is still. The words are often indistinct, but it sounds as if she is having a spirited conversation with someone whose voice is not heard. It is said that the voice is that of a woman who drowned in the lake in the 1980s. A concise history of the tragic event is not available, but a campus guard told me that the victim was a faculty member who used to swim in the lake. One day, while swimming in the cold water of spring, her strength gave out or she was disabled by cramps and she drowned.

The lake is large enough that it is unlikely a ghost hunter will hear the voice of a living being on the opposite shore. But it is important to thoroughly check out the area to make certain none of the morning joggers, walkers, or bird watchers are nearby and are creating the auditory phenomena you experience. If you are lucky, you may catch a glimpse of the female apparition. She has been seen hovering over the water, ten to twenty feet offshore, surrounded by a fog or mist.

GHOSTS OF THE INSANE ASYLUM

Western State Asylum Hospital
9601 Steilacoom Boulevard
Lakewood 98498-7213
253-582-8900

Mental-health hospitals, insane asylums, and institutions for the criminally insane are good places to hunt ghosts. Naturally, facilities that currently treat patients are not generally accessible to the public, and ghost hunters should not enter such places without explicit

The grounds of the Western State Asylum include a cemetery for patients who died at the facility. Ghosts are known to linger there over unmarked graves.

permission. But buildings that formerly housed institutions of this kind are well known for ghostly activity. The Western State Hospital in Tacoma is a large and very active facility for people with mental illnesses and those who must deal with family mental-health issues. But some of the grounds and older buildings that are no longer used by the hospital for clinical activities have been the focus of ghost hunts.

An interesting question seldom considered by paranormal investigators and ghost hunters is the mental status of a spirit. Do people who die while institutionalized for mental illness continue to be mentally ill when they become ghosts? Does death rid us of our mental peculiarities, neuroses, psychoses, and insanity? Ghost hunters who visit the Western State Hospital should consider these questions before seeking the spirits who haunt this place.

The Western State Asylum was established on Fort Steilacoom land in 1870. The first patients were admitted to the hospital in August 1871. In 1875, the state legislature renamed it the Hospital for the Insane in the Washington Territory. Dr. John W. Waughop, superintendent from 1880 to 1887, expanded the facility, its services, and bed capacity and oversaw development of farms, shops, and other facilities.

From 1876 to 1952, patients who died on the premises were buried in graves marked only with a small stone engraved with a number. Only a few traditional headstones were placed that contained the names of the deceased. Official records indicate that 2,777 graves were placed there, although there may be as many as 3,200 graves, some of which are unmarked. Most contain cremated remains. The names of those buried there remain a secret that cannot be penetrated even by the federal Freedom of Information Act. The fact that the deceased were mentally ill is the basis of their continued anonymity. And, it may also be the basis of the high frequency of ghostly activity at the graveyard and nearby barn where some headstones are kept.

The Western State Hospital cemetery is accessible by roads that traverse the vast facility. AGHOST has staged ghost hunts there that yielded interesting results. Some sensitives and psychics in the group detected the presence of several spirits who did not realize they were dead wandering the graveyard. This may be the result of their mental illness, mental deficiencies, or simply a lack of predeath connection with the body that allows a postdeath recognition of the body's death. One member of AGHOST encountered the spirit of a thirty-five-year-old man who was unhappy with his stay at the hospital and complaining that no one would give him a razor for shaving. Ghost hunters have captured orbs on film and on digital media, and mists appear when climatic conditions do not generate fog throughout the grounds. These isolated cells of mist are called ectoplasm. Also, electromagnetic field detectors have identified several hot spots or technical "hits."

Cemetery ghosts are often looking for their bodies or some information about their identities when they were alive. After death, they may have gained a "normal" mental status or at least sufficient mental function to understand their new existence and to discover they have questions about their lives and how they died. Ghost hunters who use a psychic approach may find this a useful tact when they try to contact these ghosts.

The cemetery is located behind wards K, L, and M. Look for the big red barn. Inside, displaced headstones are stored. The barn is the venue for an annual event staged in October to generate support for the cemetery and commemorate those buried anonymously on the grounds.

Another spiritually active place is a building known as the Hill Ward or the White House. The latter name is derived from the federal style of architecture, complete with columns and ornate detail at the roof line. The building is located in the rear area of the sprawling facility and surrounded by a fence. In November 2005, the building looked like a bombed-out relic from World War II. Its condition is reportedly the result of military and SWAT team exercises. The building was constructed as a dormitory for asylum inmates who worked on the hospital farm. It is unknown how many inmates died in this building, but over the course of several decades, it is likely that many passed away there.

When AGHOST members ventured inside, they found images and words on the walls that appeared to be inscribed with blood. It was reported that the surrounding fence shakes as if an unseen being were trying to escape confinement. Also, from a vantage point outside the building, ghost hunters have captured orbs on film, felt intense cold spots, and heard disembodied voices.

If you visit this site, you must not enter patient treatment areas, offices, lobbies, or other facilities currently in use. It is best to stage first your visit during daylight hours to become familiar with the grounds.

THORNEWOOD CASTLE INN AND GARDENS

8601 North Thorne Lane Southwest
Lakewood 98498
253-584-4393
www.thornewoodcastle.com

This huge mansion at the edge of American Lake may look familiar. It was featured in the 2003 Stephen King miniseries *The Diary of Ellen Rimbauer: Life at Rose Red* broadcast on ABC. The house was the perfect venue for this creepy story. Massive in size with ornate English Tudor and Gothic architectural features, its tall chimneys, many gables, doors salvaged from ancient European castles, seven-hundred-year-old windows, and parapets make this house a genuine castle complete with eerie shadows. Thornewood Castle even has ghosts that are not shy about meeting visitors and overnight guests at the popular bed-and-breakfast inn.

Thornewood Castle was built between 1907 and 1911 by Chester Thorne. Enamored by European architecture of the Middle Ages, Thorne used much of his great wealth to purchase a four-hundred-year-old Elizabethan manor which he dismantled, shipped to Washington, and reassembled as the core of his great mansion. He added doors, windows, fireplace surrounds and mantles, stonework, and many other period features to the project and created a home of twenty-seven thousand square feet with fifty-four rooms.

A curious feature of the construction project was that all the work, from foundation to roof, was done by a team of Indians. These workers, sensing that such a huge house needed charms to protect it from evil spirits, hung wishbone-shaped twigs from the ceiling and walls of the basement. The power of these charms was renewed by Indians who conducted a smudging ceremony in October 2004. The charms may have brought good fortune and protection to the house and most of its occupants, but some tragic events occurred there that are linked to hauntings and ghostly activity.

Chester Thorne died in the house on October 16, 1927, but he has been unable or unwilling to leave his spectacular mansion. After pouring millions of dollars into constructing and furnishing the place and raising a family there, it is no surprise that Thorne makes appearances at several locations within the house, making certain everything meets his approval. Thorne's ghost is a transparent apparition, without legs from the knees down, wearing a high collar, necktie, and round-rim glasses.

The ghost of Thornes' wife, Anna, shows up frequently as well. Guests and house staff have seen her sitting on the window seat in her bedroom overlooking the garden. Her image also appears in mirrors throughout the house, especially in the Bridal Suite. The Thornes' son-in-law also makes ghostly appearances. One of the many fascinating legends about Thornewood Castle tells of this brooding young man who, for unknown reasons, stepped into the large gun closet and shot himself. This ghost opens and closes doors and cabinets on the first floor.

Some time in the 1930s, the granddaughter of the next owner of Thornewood Castle drowned in the lake. Guests looking out the second-floor windows have spotted an unattended little girl walking near the beach. Concerned with her safety, they run downstairs and head to the beach, but find no one there. Others have encountered this little ghost in early morning hours or at dusk walking alone near the water's edge of the pier.

It is suspected that the Indians who built the place knew something about the land that might be a threat to the house or its occupants. Perhaps the castle sits on the site of a former village, burial ground, or location reserved for spirits. The wishbone sticks placed in the basement in 1911 may be a sign that local Indians believed otherworld entities occupied the location or often passed through it and that luck and good fortune would be needed by Chester Thorne and his descendents if they were to live in peace with these spirits.

BLACK DIAMOND CEMETERY

Morgan Street at Terrace Place
Black Diamond 98010
E-mail: bdmuseum@foxinternet.com

Cemeteries are good places to hunt for ghosts and experience a variety of paranormal activities. This is because some spirits feel a need to stay close to their bodies or close to headstones that display their names, birth dates, and other information. Having that information close at hand probably reduces their confusion about the new level of existence they experience. In some cases, spirits stay in the cemetery awaiting family members or they stay close to the grave of a loved one hoping to be reunited.

Some ghost hunters, however, have asked the question, "If you were dead, would you want to hang out for decades in a graveyard that might be overgrown with weeds?" If the spirit feels a strong tie to a place, an identity, or another individual, it might just wait no matter how unappealing the surroundings. Also, if the spirit is confused about its existence or sees the cemetery as a paradise, when in fact it is full of untended graves, weeds, refuse, and crumbling headstones, it might stay for centuries.

Black Diamond Cemetery, near the town of Black Diamond, seems to be full of spirits waiting for something or someone. The cemetery was established soon after the nearby coal mine was opened in the mid-1880s. Coal mining is dangerous work, and the first fatality occurred three months after the mine began production. Miners and their families were interred there, perhaps with a few animals.

The history of the Black Diamond Mining Co. is a curious one. The company first established a productive mine near the town of Clayton, California, about twenty miles east of San Francisco Bay. Miners and their families lived in the company town called Nortonville, which included such amenities as a store, doctor's office, and school. Nortonville's cemetery filled quickly with miners. The town's midwife, Granny Norton, was also buried there. When the mine played out in the late 1870s, the company packed up and traveled to Washington, where a rich coal deposit had been discovered in the foothills of the Cascade Mountains. The living folks moved on, leaving their dead loved ones in untended graves.

By the end of the nineteenth century, the Rose Hill Cemetery at California's Black Diamond Mine had a reputation as a strange place. The area had no wild game, and new settlers in the region refused to bury their dead there. So many ghost sightings and other paranormal events have been experienced in the graveyard. The list includes vengeful entities, huge black clouds, unexplained illness among visitors, and suicides. More than one hundred exorcisms and other ceremonies have been conducted at the cemetery to quiet the spirits or send them on to the next world.

The many sightings and ghost experiences reported at Black Diamond Cemetery suggest that this graveyard may have a spiritual nature similar to the one in California. There may be something about the tight-knit mining community of Welsh and Irish workers, their dangerous work, and their religious practices, that led to the accumulation of so many ghosts in such a small area.

Ghost hunters who visit Black Diamond Cemetery seldom fail to capture orbs on film or on digital media. Many visitors also capture strange lights that resemble miners' lanterns. These lights swing back and forth as they move across the grounds, as though a miner is swinging his lantern in search of someone or something. A white horse has also been spotted in the cemetery. It trots among the crumbling headstones, leaving a trail of dust.

Many ghost hunters visit cemeteries such as this one at night with the assumption that ghosts are easier to detect when it is dark. But ghosts have been spotted at the Black Diamond Cemetery in broad daylight. Near the far end of the cemetery, some visitors have spotted the partial apparition of a female ghost at a grave surrounded by a cast-iron fence. She faces the grave, showing only the back of her head and part of her shoulders. Her head is covered by a lace scarf that hangs down her back. If you see this ghost, she will vanish if you try to change your vantage point.

If you plan to visit this cemetery, you should stop at Black Diamond Historical Museum in the town of Black Diamond. This interesting museum is only a short distance east of the graveyard at 32627 Railroad Avenue. You may find photographs and other information that may help you research a ghost.

Other places south of Seattle to search for ghosts:

Oberlin Congregational Church

1515 Lafayette
Steilacoom 98388
253-584-4623

Immaculate Conception Catholic Mission

Nisqually at Main Street
Steilacoom 98388

Nathaniel Orr Pioneer Home Site

1811 Rainer Street
Steilacoom 98388
253-584-4133

Enumclaw Cemetery

23717 Southeast 416th Street
Enumclaw 98022
360-825-2633

Artcore Tattoo Studios

5501 Airport Way
Seattle 98108
206-767-2673

CHAPTER 4

Central Seattle and Capitol Hill

Visitors to Seattle remark how similar the city seems to San Francisco. But the emerald city on Puget Sound has its own unique charms, beautiful scenery, fascinating neighborhoods, history linked to a gold rush, and a lot of ghosts. A good way to get oriented to Seattle's history and its ghosts is to take one of the following tours: Underground Tour, Pike Place Market Ghost Tour, or Seattle Ghost Tour. (See Appendix D.) All of these can be done in one day. A short distance from central Seattle is the Capitol Hill community. The narrow, tree-lined streets, stately old homes, and buildings with documented spirits will keep ghost hunters busy and fascinated.

GHOSTS IN SEARCH OF THEIR BODIES

Former Old Seattle Cemetery
Denny Park
Denny Way at Dexter Avenue North
Seattle 98109

Cemeteries are always good places to stage ghost hunts. But spirits may be easier to find if ghost hunters visit buildings, parks, or other facilities that sit atop former cemeteries. This is particularly true if the transition of the land from a graveyard to another use was made several decades after the first graves were established, leading to a greater chance that older graves were overlooked and left behind during the relocation process. The absence of surviving relatives who care about the disposition of the remains can result in lost corpses.

Also, the failure to find more graves can be attributed to vague or inaccurate information about the location of specific graves, unmarked graves, graves with unreadable headstones, or poor oversight of the relocation process. The net result is that some of the dearly departed are left behind only to be covered with asphalt, concrete, or landscaping.

The pressure to develop valuable land, coupled with a failure to recognize important social and archeological artifacts, has resulted in the desecration of some Indian burial grounds. As a result, Indian spirits have been awakened and drawn to whatever new structure sits atop their graves. Untended, overgrown, and forgotten cemeteries in a lot of older cities have suffered a similar fate, arousing the indignation of the offended spirits.

Denny Park is a peaceful place that was once the site of Seattle's largest cemetery. Established in 1861 on land donated by David Denny, the cemetery was first occupied with bodies relocated from scattered graveyards that stood in the way of the city's development. It was believed that this patch of ground was far enough from town that it would not hinder the city's rapid expansion. From 1861 to 1884, more than 225 people were buried in that cemetery. Much later, the site was discovered to have also been an Indian burial ground that contained hundreds of remains.

By 1884, Seattle had grown so much that relocation of the cemetery became necessary. Contractor O. C. Shorey was hired to remove 223 graves and relocate them to other cemeteries. The work was difficult because many wooden grave markers had been destroyed. In addition, many markers had become unreadable by a fire that swept through the area a few years earlier. When Shorey completed the project, he reported to the Cemetery Commission that he would not be surprised if he had missed quite a few graves. In fact, when the land was regraded in the 1890s and again in the 1920s, many bodies of Seattle pioneers and Indians turned up. The remains were removed during the night to avoid upsetting area residents who had become superstitious about the land that had been used as a park since 1884.

The park that sits at this location today—named for Denny, who originally donated land for a graveyard—has been regraded to a depth of sixty feet, hopefully removing all lost headstones, marker fragments, scattered remains, and other remnants. But the disruptive process seems to have disturbed the spirits of the cemetery's former occupants.

Many people who live or work in the area believe that ghosts of Seattle pioneers and Indians roam about the park searching for their graves and their cherished remains. Visitors to the park may catch a glimpse of a partial apparition, feel cold spots or icy breezes, or capture ghostly images on film. Many ghost hunters have found orbs in their photographs and digital images.

The open space at the center of the park is a good location to start a ghost hunt. The grave of a well-known madam, Mary Conklin (1802-1873), was supposedly placed at the center of the old cemetery. Conklin was known as Damnable Mary because of her skill with profanity. When Conklin's coffin was raised in 1884, six strong men could barely lift it. Curiosity ran high as rumors spread that she might have been buried with her gold. When the workers opened her coffin, they discovered her body had turned to stone, probably a calcification process. According to official reports, they found no gold or other valuables with the strange corpse. Ghost hunters who seek the spirit of the stone madam might have some luck.

MOORE THEATRE

1932 Second Avenue at Virginia
Seattle 98121
206-467-5510

Old theaters are like time capsules that reveal a distant age when performers and audiences came together in elegant surroundings. When the Moore Theatre opened in 1907, it contained the best of these features and impressed 2,500 of Seattle's finest citizens as a great example of contemporary theater architecture in America. The stylish art included carved wooden doors and banisters, stained glass, mosaic floors and ceilings, sculpted metal light fixtures, and rich upholstery.

Some of the most popular performers in the country performed there, including Sarah Bernhardt, Marie Dressler and the Barrymores. Over many decades of service, the theater lost its luster as it was modified for boxing events, revival meetings, and other activities on the fringe of the entertainment industry. By the late 1940s, the place had fallen into disrepair. But a series of renovations that began in 1974 have returned the Moore Theatre to its former glory.

With this kind of history, it is no wonder that many people believe the theater is haunted. In fact, years ago some employees held a séance in the theater late one night in an effort to contact a spirit that haunted the theater. Some employees had reported that a male presence created the sound of heavy breathing and frightened people who worked late in the theater. The séance ended abruptly when the theater owner discovered the employees engaged in a ritual he believed to be ridiculous. By all accounts, the ghost those people sought still roams the aisles and backstage areas of the Moore Theatre.

The sound of heavy breathing seems to be this ghost's primary method of manifesting on our plane. The sound is heard from behind, as if a large, unseen being is sneaking up on you. Some theater staff have heard disembodied footsteps, too. There are no reports of apparitions, but this ghost can move objects. Small items such as keys, pens, and mobile phones, if left unattended, are found in a different location within the Moore Theatre.

The manager may permit ghost hunters to visit the theater during daylight hours if they clearly outline a plan for their investigation. Otherwise, the Moore Theatre has several interesting performers booked throughout the year, and by attending an evening performance, ghost hunters might pick up on some of the lingering charm of the theater experience as it was in 1907.

HOTEL ANDRA

2000 Fourth Street
Seattle 98121
877-448-8600 or 206-448-8600
www.hotelandra.com

The Hotel Andra is a sleek, modern place that doesn't have the look of a haunted hotel. The stylish Danish modern décor and warm atmosphere is totally opposite from the spooky atmosphere of places like Manresa Castle in Port Townsend. But the Hotel Andra occupies a building with a curious history, and it has ghosts.

Built in 1926 as an upscale hotel, it slipped into disrepair by the late 1930s. For a while, the building was little more than a flophouse and probably harbored a number of gamblers, drug addicts, terminal alcoholics, and others who had simply run out of luck. In the 1950s and 1960s, things started to turn around as central Seattle underwent an urban renewal. The brick and terra-cotta exterior was cleaned up and repaired, and the place was reopened as the Claremont Hotel. As the surrounding neighborhood developed a reputation for its galleries, restaurants, boutiques, and art studios, the hotel became more popular with travelers. In 2004, the building underwent another major remodeling to give it the northwest ambience for which the Hotel Andra is known.

The hotel is also known for its ghosts. Guests have complained of hearing loud parties, usually on Friday and Saturday nights. The sounds give the impression of a wild 1920s party with a jazz band, riotous laughing, and stomping feet. Even the sounds of breaking glass, like windows and drinking glasses, have been heard as the party reaches its peak. Most of the complaints come from guests who stay on the ninth floor. Those who stay on the floor below sometimes hear the ghostly party, too. Naturally, when hotel staff members investigate the complaints, they find no signs of a party. A short time after the staff members return to the front desk, the loud party resumes.

Visitors to the lobby and the Lola bar, at the corner of the hotel's ground floor, have witnessed objects floating around the room as if held by invisible hands. Some reports say objects even fly off tables.

Hotel staff may tell you the story of a maintenance worker who lost her life when she fell from a stool or ladder. This tragic event occurred in the 1960s in one of the guest rooms on the ninth floor. The woman was new to the hotel and had been hanging curtains late in the evening. She may have been startled by the noise of a 1920s party or by the ghost of a hotel guest who committed suicide in a room on the eighth floor. Her ghost is believed to be responsible for the unexplained movement of curtains and drapes in many rooms on the upper floors.

A HOST OF GHOSTS

Rivoli Apartment Building
2127 Second Avenue
Seattle 98121-2214

This three-story brick apartment building is a very spooky place. Ghost hunters may enter the Rivoli only with the permission of the manager or a resident. Always respect the security barriers of a building and the privacy of its residents. The building has many fascinating architectural features including the Byzantine-style terra-cotta surround at the entry. If you gain lawful entry, you may see several ghosts there. During the years when the building had lost its charm due to poor maintenance and general wear and tear, several people died there. Two men died of AIDS. A young Eskimo woman was murdered, an older man committed suicide, and a middle-aged alcoholic woman with a mental illness died of unknown causes. The ghosts of these people are often seen in the apartments and hallways of the Rivoli.

A woman in her late thirties or early forties named Christine died in a third-floor apartment in the mid-1980s. She was well known to social workers who, it is said, tried to get her to move from the Rivoli to a residential facility where she could receive the help and therapy she needed. With few visitors and no friends, Christine used to clog her toilet so the building's maintenance man would spend some time with her in her apartment. Long after her death, Christine still instigates plumbing problems at the Rivoli. Anytime a drain is stopped up, a toilet malfunctions, or a sink overflows, Christine's ghost shows up to greet the plumber. Residents of the Rivoli have also seen this ghost, who has straight brown hair and a rotund body.

Visitors have also spotted apparitions of the AIDS victims and the man who killed himself, usually in the hallways or on the back stairs.

Decades ago, wild times in the Rivoli Apartment Building produced several ghosts.

They have reported that one of these men gazes at passersby on the street through the glass of the double front doors.

The best known ghost at the Rivoli is a young Eskimo woman. Reports say that she arrived in Seattle in the early 1980s, hoping to start a new life, one with more opportunities than she faced in her native village. Unfortunately, the woman fell in love with a hot-blooded, mentally ill Cuban named Rodolfo. A brief and stormy relationship ended when, in a jealous rage, Rodolfo stabbed his girlfriend, thinking she had been unfaithful to him. In order to avoid a murder rap, the Cuban stuffed the woman's body in a Murphy bed, one that folds into the wall. Then, he paid a month's rent in advance, padlocked the apartment door, and left town. Weeks later, people began to notice a strange smell, and complaints were made to the manager. When he opened the apartment, the horrible stench and blood-stained bedding triggered a thorough search, and the woman's body was discovered. Not long after the victim's body was removed, residents heard the voices of the Cuban and Eskimo arguing and detected the foul odor of the rotting corpse.

The unfortunate Eskimo woman still walks the hallways of the Rivoli. Perhaps her fervent dreams of a new life were so strong that they have kept her spirit in Seattle long after her death.

SORRENTO HOTEL

900 Madison Street
Seattle 98104-1234
206-622-6400

It might be the location that makes this fancy hotel a gathering place for ghosts. The Sorrento Hotel sits across the street from a blood bank, less than half a block from the emergency entrance of a hospital, and only two blocks from a huge medical center. Or it may be the attractive European opulence of the hotel, including a spectacular sitting room off the main entrance and the Hunt Club bar that attracts spirits with a taste for classy accommodations.

For many years, the Hunt Club bar has been known as a place where strange things happen, even during daylight hours. The stylish, dark décor and subdued lighting create a congenial atmosphere that makes patrons forget the time of day and allows ghosts to move about without much notice. But cold spots, icy breezes, and sensations that an invisible being is standing close by are often experienced there. You may slip into a booth with a friend but feel that the cozy spot is strangely crowded. Some patrons have witnessed glasses moving around on the bar. It usually happens when a customer leaves his seat to make a phone call or visit the restroom. While his drink sits unattended, a ghost moves it about as if it is trying to steal a sip. Sometimes, wine glasses slide on the bar as much as twelve inches.

On the fourth floor, near room 408, the partial apparition of an older woman has been seen. She appears out of nowhere, walks eight to ten feet, and then vanishes as she arrives in front of room 408. One hotel staff member said that an out-of-town woman died in that room after attending the funeral of her childhood sweetheart.

Off the lobby, a large round sitting room takes visitors back to the late Victorian atmosphere of 1911, the year the hotel opened. Palm trees, carved wood trim, large mirrors, a baby grand piano, and a mosaic fireplace surround attract guests and ghosts alike. I visited this sitting room in November 2005 and found a woman sitting in a chair next to the fireplace. Apparently, she noticed me as I took photographs of the mosaic surround. As I got closer to her, she asked, "Do you want me to move?" After replying, "No, thank you," I turned away, wishing not to disturb a hotel guest. I turned to glance back, the woman was gone. If this woman was a ghost, she was completely lifelike, but her voice lacked energy. Her words were spoken almost in a whisper.

GHOSTS OF THE UNDERGROUND CITY

Entrance at Doc Maynard's Public House
Pioneer Square
608 First Avenue
Seattle 98104
206-682-4646
www.undergroundtour.com

Pioneer Square, Doc Maynard's Public House, and the remains of Seattle's underground city are essential experiences for ghost hunters who explore this fascinating city. The story behind the underground city is unique and much too complex to be presented here. However, some background material will be useful to anyone who ventures below street level in search of ghosts.

From the day the city was founded in 1851, the tide had a strong effect on the town. Built on mudflats traversed by hundreds of streams and estuaries, the streets of Seattle were rarely passable without mud clinging to boots or dirt flying into the air from the wheels of passing wagons. The popular solution was to build on stilts, keeping hotels, flophouses, bars, and stores above the high-tide mark and away from anything unsavory that might be floating in the brown water. Also, some sidewalks and streets were constructed from huge planks. The vast array of wooden structures was literally a pile of matchsticks awaiting ignition. And ignition happened on June 6, 1889. The failure of the town's makeshift water system and other calamities resulted in the destruction of thirty-six blocks of buildings at a cost of fifteen million dollars.

The urge to rebuild was strong among the people and their politicians, but these two groups didn't coordinate their efforts. The politicians and investment banks wanted to raise the streets to avoid tidal intrusion, sewage problems, and reduce drainage problems during heavy rains that had plagued the city since its founding. Their plans, however, were complex and required a lot of engineering and planning. Merchants and others could not wait years for that to happen, so they rebuilt their properties as fast as possible and reopened for business. By the time the city started work on the streets, many hotels, bars and restaurants were back in business.

Eventually, city engineers got to work and raised street levels as much as thirty-two feet by constructing retaining walls at the edge of old sidewalks and backfilling. The result was likened to a waffle, where the ridges represented the streets of new Seattle and the depressions represented the land on which most of the businesses sat. The result was awkward—and sometimes dangerous—and created a lot of problems. Passersby on the streets could not easily access businesses. In fact, as many as seventeen men fell to their deaths while negotiating the tricky elevated streets. Ladders had to be installed at every corner so citizens could descend to the old street level to enter a hotel or store.

Over time, merchants realized that what was once their second floor should become their ground floor to facilitate entry of customers from the new, elevated street level. Buildings that were restored after the fire, as well as newly built structures, made the necessary architectural concession. Former ground-floor spaces became basements. Eventually, those basements became places where residents could find illegal or immoral businesses, thus becoming well-known dens of iniquity. Gambling, prostitution, opium dens, and Shanghai bars flourished just as respectable businesses on the new street level regained a footing and started to turn a profit.

When word of the illicit underground businesses spread far

enough to irritate the delicate sensibilities of the town's politicians and upper crust, many demanded action. The action was to tax the disreputable businesses rather than eradicate them. Many of the women engaged in prostitution were referred to as seamstresses. So, a sewing machine tax was levied that funded various civic improvements.

Eventually, the underground portions of many buildings were overrun by bums, criminals, derelicts, and rats carrying bubonic plague and the operators of illegitimate gambling halls and bars left for more congenial facilities. By 1930, Seattle's underground city had been forgotten and completely overrun by rats, sewage overflow, and insects.

This treasure trove of early Seattle history was reopened by writer and entrepreneur Bill Speidel in 1964. Speidel aroused the interest of Seattle's citizens, many of whom refused to believe stories of a forgotten city beneath the streets of modern Seattle. When access to the old sidewalks and storefronts was finally secured in May 1965, five hundred people showed up for the first tour. Since then, the underground tour of old Seattle has become one of the biggest attractions in the western U.S. The official entry to the underground city is through Doc Maynard's Public House. Visitors must purchase tickets and tour with a group led by a knowledgeable and entertaining guide. Tour groups can be large—as many as forty—but there is plenty of room and opportunity for ghost hunters to look for spirits and environmental imprints, along with experiencing some of the paranormal phenomena that goes on there.

With a history of unsavory businesses conducted in the dim light of an underground city, it is no surprise that many parts of subterranean Seattle harbor ghosts. But ghost hunters may encounter a spirit even before descending beneath the streets of Seattle. A dark specter hangs out in the café/bar located on the first floor of Doc Maynard's Public House. The building dates from 1890 and housed many businesses, including bars, gambling halls, and brothels, so it isn't clear where this spirit comes from. It is clear, though, that it doesn't like the music played on the modern jukebox. Patrons who play some offensive rock tune may see condiment bottles scoot across the surface of a table and fall to the floor. In fact, there are

Seattle's underground tour includes this former teller's cage, where the ghost of an elderly banker appears.

few choices on the jukebox player that please this ghost.

When you descend fourteen feet below the modern streets of Seattle, you will instantly feel transported to a past century. The dim, dusty remains of window frames and doorways, old brick-paved sidewalks, discarded furniture, and machinery are good reminders of a past era. Rats even scamper about in this very strange place. Tour guides may mention places where ghosts have been seen, but your best opportunity to spot one of them is to walk at the front or far end of the group.

The ghost of an elderly gentleman is often seen standing outside the bank vault. Tour guides, visitors, psychics, and ghost hunters have spotted this lifelike ghost. He has been described as five foot eleven to six foot one, with brown hair parted on the left side. His long mustache extends to his cheeks. He is dressed in late-nineteenth-century clothing, including a white shirt with sleeves rolled up, a band collar without a tie, and brown twill pants. This ghost doesn't speak, but he gives every impression that he is very much alive. In fact, some visitors think this man is a costumed reenactor or member of the tour staff.

The bank ghost may be a teller or manager still looking after the millions of dollars in gold that passed through Seattle during the Alaska gold rush of 1898. Ghost hunters should also stand in the teller's cage. Intense cold spots have been found there. Photographers often find orbs in their pictures.

A room full of ghosts may be found in the Korn Building. Tour guides usually pause in this large subterranean room to tell stories of gambling, prostitution, and all the other vices that went on here. The room still has some discarded furniture, light fixtures, and architectural features that help ghost hunters get in touch with the past era. If you step away from the group, you may pick up on paranormal remnants from the wild days when this place was a barroom and dance hall. I encountered the boisterous laughing of several unseen people, the smell of whiskey, and the tinkling of a honky-tonk piano.

Ghost hunters have spotted several Indians throughout the underground city. Perhaps old Seattle was built over an Indian burial ground or a place where Indians had died. A group of three Indian ghosts have been seen near the exit from the underground city.

GHOSTS OF THE LYNCHED INDIANS

First Street and Main
Seattle 98104

At several locations in Seattle, spirits of Indians who lived on the shores of Puget Sound have been discovered by ghost hunters.

Intertribal warfare, starvation during harsh winters, conflicts with white settlers, and fights with sailors and others passing through on their way to the Yukon gold rush all contributed to the passing of the Indians from the city. But at Pioneer Square in 1854, Chief Seattle elegantly reminded Governor Stevens, and several others who founded the city, that his people would never truly be gone from their cherished homeland.

"And when the last red man shall have perished from the earth and his memory among white men shall have become a myth, these shores shall swarm with the invisible dead of my tribe, and when your children's children shall think themselves alone in the field, the store, the shop, upon the highway or in the silence of the woods, they will not be alone."

With these prophetic words, Chief Seattle reminds us that the ghosts of his people still walk among us. So it isn't any wonder that locals, tourists, and those passing through the old downtown district have felt strange sensations in Pioneer Square and another location two short blocks from there.

In April 1854, three Indians were accused of murdering a tradesman from Pennsylvania. His body was discovered in a shallow grave on the beach at Lake Union, and somehow the Indians were linked to his death. With little in the way of due process of law, two of the Indians were apprehended and dragged to Pioneer Square, where a mob hastily convened a court. Within minutes, they were found guilty and then dragged two blocks to First Street and Main, where a tree stood suitable for a double hanging. Standing firmly against the mob, the local sheriff held the third Indian. That man was later tried in a regular court and found not guilty. This verdict raises the suspicion that the two who were hanged might also have been found not guilty had they been lucky enough to make their way to a well-guarded court.

Sensitive ghost hunters and psychics sometimes encounter unseen spirits at the corner of First, as well as at Main and Pioneer Square. An odd rush of air, counter to the usual prevailing breeze, and other spirit manifestations may be residual environmental imprints of the angry lynch mob. Some have suggested that the rush of air could be from the frightened Indians or the guilt of citizens who watched the illegal proceedings in horror. A stump that sits among the ferns in

Pioneer Square is said to be the hanging stump on which the two Indians, and other victims of lynch mobs, stood as they drew their last breaths before the nooses were drawn tight.

GHOST OF THE INDIAN PRINCESS

Pike Place Public Market
1529 Pike Place
Seattle 98101-3523
206-624-8082

The history of Pike Place Public Market is really a microcosm of Seattle politics and civic-renewal policies of the early and mid-twentieth century. The market is also a popular shopping place for locals and a unique attraction for tourists. More than nine million tourists visit the collection of shops each year. Added to all that, the market place is haunted. Its history spans more than one hundred years and includes at least one brothel and a World War II dance hall, plus passionate architects, ardent preservationists, centuries-old buildings placed on Indian burial grounds, and Japanese merchants displaced by relocation and internment during World War II. No wonder the seventeen-acre market place is haunted by many ghosts.

The most famous ghost of Pike Place Public Market is the Indian princess Angelina. She has been spotted by many ghost hunters and others who happened to see the entity when they least expected to have a paranormal experience. Michael Yaeger, owner of a shop in the market place, described Princess Angelina as short and slim, dressed in pale white Indian clothing, and having the bluest eyes he had ever seen. The spirit appears in full detail, but the apparition is transparent except for the intense blue eyes.

Princess Angelina was one of Chief Seattle's daughters. Her date of birth is unknown, but photographs of her taken in the early 1890s show her as a frail-looking elderly woman. In her later years she was a familiar figure on Seattle's waterfront near the site of the present-day Pike Place Public Market. Princess Angelina lived in a small shack built on stilts surrounded by mudflats, where she dug clams. Apparently, she sustained herself by digging clams and selling them to passersby at a site where the market stands today.

Photographer Edward S. Curtis often saw Angelina on the streets and struck up a friendship with her. Intrigued by the princess, he paid her one dollar for each photograph he took of her. Angelina was happy with the arrangement, and she often said that she preferred sitting for photographs rather than digging for clams.

Curtis's photographs of Princess Angelina can be found on the Internet. In several photos she appears ill and destitute. The appearance of this elderly Indian princess who peddled clams to the white citizens is hard to reconcile with the high esteem the people of Seattle had for her father, Chief Seattle.

The ghost of Princess Angelina seems to have a strong interest in the land and the market that sits on the bluff overlooking Puget Sound. She usually appears after the shops close for the night. As shopkeepers and maintenance people carry out their late-night jobs, she wanders the passageways, looking things over or making her rounds to sell clams. By many accounts, her pale white transparent clothing appears like a fog, but her bright blue eyes are lifelike and full of energy. A ghost tour of Pike Place Public Market conducted by Mercedes Yaeger of Market Ghost Tours is the best way to have a face-to-face meeting with Princess Angelina.

Market developer Arthur Goodwin's ghost has been seen by many merchants at several locations throughout the market place, particularly the Goodwin Library, room 314 on the upper floor. In 1926, Arthur succeeded his uncle, Frank Goodwin, as principle investor in market operations, which meant he called all the shots. Frank's ghost appears at several places in the market and looks so lifelike that he is easily recognized by old timers and those familiar with his likeness from historical photographs. Only the upper half of Frank Goodwin's body is visible. The apparition appears with a serious gaze in his eyes, as if he is critically looking over a store's design or inventory or the skill of the people working there. After a few seconds of his icy stare, the ghost vanishes. Frank Goodwin's ghost has been reported in spaces on the upper floor that used to be his office. The space now houses the Goodwin Library.

In a store called the Bead Emporium, the ghost of a child unravels strings of beads and lets them scatter on the floor. Sometimes, this mischievous spirit throws beads or other trinkets at customers. It is likely that this ghost lived in the space now occupied by the store or spent many hours each day at the site while his parents operated a business. A clue was discovered when a wall was opened during renovations. Little baskets of beads were found in a space that would be accessible only during construction. Renovations done in the 1920s or 1930s offered a brief opportunity for a little boy to hide his beads inside a wall. Some time after his death, he returned to the site to search for his stash. He must have been thrilled to find an entire store filled with beads, baubles, and trinkets because this kid likes to handle the merchandise and leave it scattered.

At Shakespeare Books, Suite 326, a ghost throws a book off the shelf nearly every night. For several months, the same book was found in the same spot on the floor each morning. When the exasperated store manager threw the book away, the ghost started heaving another book. A few sensitive visitors have seen this ghost. Many

The historic Pike Place Public Market is home to the ghost of an Indian princess as well as that of the market's founders.

others have attempted to establish a psychic connection or at least communicate with it.

During World War II, the Boeing Aircraft Co. staged Saturday dances in the upstairs hall to entertain its workers. One of the men who attended these dances was a tall, well-dressed fellow who was amazingly light on his feet. He danced with several women and left them all wondering why he seemed so different. As time passed, the women compared notes, and they all agreed that this fancy dancer wasn't real. He was too light, too swift on his feet, and his hand felt as light as a feather. At a reunion after the war, several women concluded that the dancer was a ghost. This fellow may still be practicing his foot work on the second floor where the dance hall used to be, even though the floor was destroyed by a fire years ago. Disembodied tapping and the sliding of dancing shoes is often heard there.

GHOSTS OF THE WAH MEE MASSACRE

Maynard Alley between South King and South Weller streets
Seattle 98104-2019

On February 18, 1983, three young men burst into the Wah Mee gambling club in Seattle's Chinatown, killed fourteen people, and walked out with tens of thousands of dollars. The brutal mass murder was one of the largest in U.S. history, leaving the Chinese community stunned and puzzled because both the perpetrators and the victims were local Chinese.

The Wah Mee was a historic speakeasy during Prohibition, but after World War II it became one of many gambling and social clubs in the growing Chinese community. The club was described as a classy, romantic enclave patronized by affluent Chinese who enjoyed good food and high-stakes gambling. On some nights, tens of thousands of dollars crossed the tables. The well-known people who frequented the Wah Mee often had a lot of cash in their pockets. This information was not lost on twenty-two-year-old Willie Mak, who had racked up a huge gambling debt with another club. In order to get the loan sharks off his back, Mak planned a robbery of the Wah

In 1983, the Wah Mee gambling club was robbed and fourteen patrons were killed. Ghost hunters have detected spiritual remnants of this tragic event.

Mee with pals Benjamin Ng and Tony Ng (no relation).

The three men entered the club just before midnight, thinking the patrons would be too drunk to put up much of a fight. They hog-tied several customers and dealers, emptied their pockets, and scooped up large sums from the tables. With their pockets brimming with cash, they opened fire, killing fourteen people. When police entered the building, the entire floor was covered with blood. One man survived the shooting. Wai Yok Chin, a sixty-two-year-old Pai Kau dealer, suffered bullet wounds to the neck, but he was able to speak clearly enough to name Willie Mak, Ben Ng, and Tony Ng as perpetrators.

Within hours, Mak and Ben Ng were apprehended by the police. Tony Ng took off for Canada, but was caught and extradited two years after the murders. Jurors found him guilty of robbery and assault, but not murder since he carried no weapon during the crime. Mak and Ben Ng each got life sentences.

The mass murder at the Wah Mee struck the very heart of the Chinese community. For many reasons, the club never reopened. Visitors to the site today find padlocked doors covered with graffiti. Permission to enter the club is tough to get, but visitors can look in a window and see if ghosts of the murder victims look back. To the left of the entrance, you may get a peak of the interior by looking through the solitary clear block that is part of a glass block wall. One way to visit this haunted site is to join the Seattle Ghost Tour. (See Appendix F.)

By all accounts, there are plenty of ghosts at this location. Some ghost hunters have seen ghosts sitting at the bar or at one of the gambling tables that still remain in the old club. Also, strong environmental imprints have been detected by sensitive ghost hunters. Apparently, a few patrons dashed for the door the moment the murderers drew their weapons. Their fear left an imprint at the front door and also at the doorway on the alley. Psychics have felt their emotions and sharp spikes in intensity that mark the firing of the murder weapons.

SPIRITS OF THE OLD MORTUARY

The Starlite Lounge Restaurant
2721 First Avenue
Seattle 98104
206-448-8826

The Starlite Lounge is a lively place, even for the dead. It offers a bit of Las Vegas with starburst chandeliers, burnt-red-colored walls and furniture, and a huge mural featuring the Rat Pack—Frank Sinatra, Sammy Davis Jr., Dean Martin, and Joey Bishop—over the bar. There is no gambling, of course, but the entertainment can satisfy your urge to get on a plane for a weekend in glitzy Las Vegas. But most patrons don't realize that a high-energy evening in the Starlite is actually an evening spent in the former chapel of one of Seattle's oldest mortuaries.

E. R. Butterworth opened his mortuary at this location in 1903. Hundreds of bodies were processed there before services were staged in the chapel. After World War II, the mortuary business moved to another location and various other businesses occupied the building. Architectural remnants of the old mortuary, though, are everywhere. At the entrance, porcelain tiles seem out of place for a nightclub, but appropriate for the funeral business. From the left to right, the mosaics include the words "private," "office," and "chapel." The doors are original and, with their oval glass inserts and decorative metal fixtures, look more fitting for a chapel or mortuary than a nightclub.

After passing through the foyer, visitors notice the overhead Byzantine terra-cotta decorative trim on what appears to be a dropped ceiling. This structure used to be the choir loft. Across the room, large faux balconies, with the same decorative detail, cling to the walls above doorways. These contribute to the churchlike atmosphere of the room, which was once used for viewing the deceased.

Ghost hunters have to look past the fancy décor, well-stocked bar, and Vegas-style lighting to see spirits of the dead whose bodies were prepared for burial, placed on display, and cremated in this building. Co-owner Steve Harris often gives ghost hunters permission to explore the basement, snap a few photographs, and check EMF meters before the club opens for business.

Partial apparitions are often seen at several spots within the building, usually dressed in early-twentieth-century clothing and looking quite pale. The owner of a restaurant that preceded the Starlite Lounge in the old mortuary once saw a procession of ghostly apparitions walk through the largest room. They were dressed in clothing from several eras and included all ethnicities. This may have been a reunion of spirits of all those who were processed for burial there.

Ghost hunters who use a technical approach may find orbs in photographs and digital images. Others have had good success with EVP (Electronic Voice Phenomena). I obtained an EVP of sobbing and the sound of something slamming shut, possibly a coffin lid.

A good approach to investigating this place is to patronize the lounge and wander about the spaces open to customers. Talk to employees about recent ghostly activity. If the place is interesting, speak to the manager about a short after-hours visit. And when you spend time at the Starlite Lounge, don't be surprised if some of the customers or staff look a little different or fail to respond to questions. You might be talking to a ghost.

The lively Starlite Lounge was once a mortuary and has the ghosts to prove it.

SUICIDE BRIDGE

Aurora Bridge, a k a George Washington Memorial Bridge (Highway 99)
Seattle 98109

Tall bridges seem to be a magnet for people intent on committing suicide. They also seem to be a magnet for the ghosts of those who met their deaths by jumping from the high span and slamming into the cold surface of the water below. The Aurora Bridge—formally named the George Washington Memorial Bridge—is just as attractive a venue for suicide as its distant cousin, the Golden Gate Bridge in San Francisco.

Built in the early 1930s, the Aurora Bridge stands 167 feet above the Lake Washington Ship Canal that connects Lake Union with Puget Sound. An average of three people jump from the bridge each year. There may be many more who leap without witnesses and whose bodies are not discovered. In August 2001, hundreds of commuters witnessed a suicide attempt. A woman climbed the side rail

Desperate people who have jumped from the Aurora Bridge have left emotional imprints on the pavement and walks.

and stood there long enough to bring motorists to a halt, causing a huge traffic jam. As drivers crept by her, some yelled, "Go ahead. Jump!" After several minutes, the woman jumped, but survived the fall. This event drew national attention, including stories on *Good Morning, America*.

Ghosts from some of the Aurora Bridge suicides still stand at the rail, contemplating eternity. Chalk marks on the cement roadbed have been seen between 2:00 a.m. and 4:00 a.m. at the spot where a man and his dog made the leap. Several astonished commuters have seen the apparition of the man and dog standing at the edge of the road.

Many people who cross the bridge at night slow down and stay in the right-hand lane, hoping to get a glimpse of one of the many ghosts regularly spotted at the rails. Some have actually seen apparitions re-create their leaps from the span. These images may be environmental imprints of intense emotions rather than the spirits of dead people.

Ghost hunters should be careful not to impede traffic on this busy highway. Also, keep in mind that most of the bridge's suicides have taken place on the north-bound side facing Lake Union.

MISTRESS OF THE ISLAND

Ruins of the Trimble Mansion
Blake Island, Puget Sound (access via private boat or tour boat)
206-933-8600 or 800-426-1205

By all accounts, wealthy real estate financier William Pitt Trimble (1863-1943) and his family lived happy and fun-filled lives until 1929. With his wife, Cassandra, and their five children, they enjoyed boating, fishing, and nature outings throughout the Puget Sound region. In 1903, they fell in love with little Blake Island, located only six miles from Seattle, and decided to make it their permanent summer destination. Trimble unraveled a complicated set of claims and false deeds and purchased the north side of the island, renaming it Trimble Island. Within a few years they had built a large house with wide verandas and sleeping porches to accommodate their many guests. The Trimbles intended the place to be a summer vacation home, but from 1917 to 1923, the family lived there year-round, with William commuting to work aboard his fifty-foot cruiser. From late spring to early fall, the place was full of guests. Sometimes they staged huge parties on weekends.

The family's idyllic lifestyle on the island came to a crashing halt on December 7, 1929, when the family's car ran off the King Street pier in Seattle and sank in Elliot Bay. Cassandra drowned inside the vehicle, but William and two of their sons, William Jr. and Ford, swam to safety. The loss was devastating, and the family never returned to Trimble Island.

Eventually, the house, gardens, tennis court, and horse pasture fell into disrepair. In 1936, William sold his portion of the island to a local investment company. With this transaction, Trimble Island became known as Blake Island once again. After the Trimble family left the island, vandals and rum runners camped out in the rapidly decaying house. They broke windows and tore up fancy woodwork for firewood. Eventually, a fire consumed the place.

William's grief over the loss of his wife was compounded by the loss of most of his financial holdings in the crash of 1929. By the late 1930s he was a mere shadow of his former self. He moved to a modest house on Capitol Hill, where he lived alone until his death in 1943.

Today, visitors to Blake Island are either hikers or bikers who enjoy the island's fifteen miles of trails. Tourists come to spend a few hours at Tillicum Village, a replica Indian longhouse where salmon dinners are served during Indian dances and other rituals. But a few of the island's one hundred thousand annual visitors venture beyond these activities to visit the remains of the Trimble house. Sensitive ghost hunters and psychics who spend a little time at the ruins have picked up several environmental imprints and recorded some EVP. Boisterous laughter of several people enjoying a great party, a disembodied woman's scream, the crash of lumber as if a roof has caved in, and a man yelling "No, no. No!" have been heard there. One psychic believes a murder was committed on the island before the great fire that destroyed the twelve-room Trimble Mansion.

Ghost hunters who visit the ruins should try EVP. Also, visitors skilled in meditation should try to pick up the environmental imprint of the great summer party. This is probably the big bash the family staged at the end of the summer in 1923.

RADISSON HOTEL

17001 Pacific Highway at 170th Avenue
Seattle 98188
206-242-9978

If you look at satellite images of this location, you will see something curious. The hotel is built on the very edge of a large cemetery. A line of tall trees marks a corner of the graveyard and continues on the other side of a small street. Not only is the species of trees in the two stands identical, but the height of all the trees is the same. This suggests that the Radisson Hotel was built on ground that was once part of Washington Memorial Park Cemetery. Some members of AGHOST suspect that a few bodies were left behind when the boundaries of the cemetery were changed to accommodate the expansion of the airport and the construction of International Boulevard and the hotel. This is a common occurrence in many cities, when expansion of existing facilities or new construction occurs rapidly, driven by intense economic pressure.

Hotel staff members and guests have reported the muted sound of two people engaged in a conversation in the hallway of the north building (closest to the cemetery). When someone opens the door to ask the people to quiet down, no one found is ever found. This has happened so often, that front-desk staff are used to getting calls from guests in the north wing. Ghost hunters have dismissed the possibility that the annoying conversation is coming through the ventilation system, from a room with the door left open, or from a TV or radio.

Often, the peculiar conversation moves down the hall as if invisible people are talking as they walk from the east end to the west end of the corridor. EVP might be obtained at this location. Ghost hunters who stay the night in the north wing might consider letting an audio recorder run for a few hours with a microphone set to pick up sound in the corridor. Mundane conversations of living guests passing through the hallway might be easy to distinguish from the conversation of dead people who died during the 1940s or earlier.

GRAND ARMY OF THE REPUBLIC CEMETERY

Twelfth Avenue East at East Howe Street
Capitol Hill District
Seattle 98102

The notion that cemetery are haunted is widely accepted because we tend to think that the spirits of the dead want to stay with their body. They do so because they cannot tear themselves away from the old, decaying flesh. Also, they may believe their current state is all a dream and that they will soon wake up. Some ghosts remain at their gravesites awaiting visits from relatives and friends whom they cannot find elsewhere. Whatever the reason and whatever the condition of the graves and grounds, there are ghosts in cemeteries.

This peaceful cemetery was opened in 1895 as a final resting place for veterans of the Civil War. Five of Seattle's Grand Army of the Republic posts established the exclusive cemetery on land donated by Huldah and David Kaufman. It contains 526 graves shaded by trees and surrounded by grassy fields. After 1922, responsibility for maintaining the grounds, including the gravestones and boundaries of the property, was divided among the city, the GAR, and the adjacent Lake View Cemetery. Naturally, this led to disarray, and the cemetery declined in the 1930s. During World War II, a unit of coast artillery was stationed on the grounds. In the 1960s, the Veterans Administration declined to take over the cemetery, so the GAR continued to care for the gravestones while the Seattle Parks and Recreation Department assumed responsibility for the grounds.

This cemetery, like most in the region, has been visited by several ghost hunters because visitors have reported strange experiences. People claim to have seen men dressed in Civil War uniforms walking around the place or hovering over a headstone. Some of them, as partial apparitions, march in unison, while others appear as solitary figures gazing at their grave markers. People who live across the street from the cemetery have reported seeing strange lights and unexplainable fogs and mists and hearing the sound of marching boots.

While in the area, ghost hunters should go across the street to visit some of Seattle's notables who lie at peace in Lake View Cemetery. Opened in 1873 as a Masonic cemetery, it contains the remains and monuments of Doc Maynard; martial artist Bruce Lee and his son, Brandon; department-store founder John Nordstrom; Milton Holgate, who was killed by Indians in the Battle of Seattle; and Arthur Denny, whose name appears on just about everything in Seattle. Also, there are several fascinating graves of Masons marked with tall Egyptian obelisks.

DARRYL THE TEENAGE GHOST

905 East Pine Street at Broadway (formerly Burnley English Institute)
Capitol Hill District
Seattle 98122-2413

Sometime in the late 1950s or early 1960s, a young man lost his life in this building. Different stories have been published by reputable writers. One tells that the 1907 building was once used as a physical-education center for a nearby high school. During one of the classes, competition ran high and a fight broke out in which a student was accidentally killed. The second story describes a despondent student who had been studying at the Burnley School of Professional Art. He died on the steep, back steps of the building, either by accident or suicide.

In either case, the entity that occupies this building has been detected by many people since the early 1960s. Henry Bennett, an artist who lived in the building for many years, reportedly heard disembodied footsteps and the sounds of furniture being moved about many times. Others have witnessed objects being pushed from the shelves by invisible hands and doors swinging open and closed. Astonished witnesses have watched as telephones were dialed and coffee was made by the mysterious, invisible entity.

Séances conducted in the 1960s confirmed that a ghost inhabited the building, but little information has been uncovered as to the ghost's identity, cause of death, or reason for haunting the building. One group of psychics, however, concluded the entity was a basketball player. The

This building is home to the ghost of a young man who lost his life in a fight.

psychics were unclear as to whether he played in pick-up games or was a member of a team. This entity conveyed that he was angry that he had died at a young age. The energy of his anger may have created the crashing and dragging sounds reported by many of the building's occupants.

Today, the ground floor of the building houses a dental clinic. The upper floors are used by Seattle Central Community College for student

An orb is visible on the step below young ghost hunter Michael Dwyer. He is in the spot where a teenager died after a fight.

meetings, tutoring, and other instructional services. In November 2005, I interviewed several people who work in the building, and they all agreed that ghostly activity occurs frequently, even during daylight hours. The area where the gym was once located is almost unrecognizable, but patches of hardwood floor and heavy overhead beams can be seen if you look for these architectural features. Be sure to obtain prior permission from the building superintendent and tenants. Also, the back stairs, believed by many to be the location of a suicide, can be viewed. These stairs are best accessed by ascending the exterior metal staircase to the second floor, then entering the building on the landing of the interior staircase.

A recent investigation of the premises by a ghost hunter who uses psychic methods yielded some interesting findings. According to this ghost hunter, the young man who died there was involved with sports. He was not an art student. A fight broke out during an informal game played with other youths from the neighborhood. The entity, whose name was perceived as Darryl or Darren, ran to the rear stairs, where his rivals caught up with him and pushed him down the stairs. People who work in the building have nicknamed this ghost Burnley.

Darryl moves throughout the building, but he is most active on the second and third floors. On the back stairs, ghost hunters may encounter hauntings or environmental imprints created by Darryl's horror as he fell to his death.

GHOSTS OF THE CHURCH PEOPLE

Capitol Hill Methodist Church Office Building
Sixteenth Avenue at John Street
Capitol Hill District
Seattle 98122
206-860-2525 or 206-826-8000

At the end of the nineteenth century, the Reverend Daniel Bagley and his charming wife, Susannah, were pillars of the small Capitol Hill community. The reverend had the good fortune to be assigned pastor of the Methodist church, and he proudly assumed the spiritual helm of the stately Gothic-style house of worship, which included a tall tower capped with a spire and cross, magnificent stained-glass windows, and graceful arches that span the sanctuary. The well-to-do community generously supported the church and filled the pews every Sunday. With even-handed sermons delivered by Daniel and a popular women's auxiliary headed by Susannah, the membership grew, and the Bagleys became important social and spiritual figures.

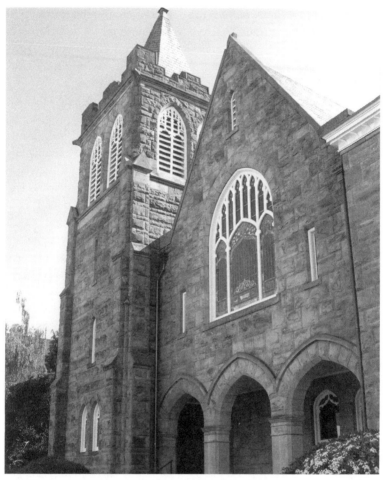

Ghosts of church people haunt this magnificent building in Capitol Hill.

It was a bit of a paradise that neither Daniel nor Susannah could ever imagine leaving, even after their deaths.

Daniel died first, followed only two years later by Susannah. Others came to keep the congregation together through two world wars, the Great Depression, and the social upheavals of the 1960s and '70s. Daniel and Susannah were present through these periods, but most certainly out of sight to most who worshiped there.

By the early 1990s, social issues divided the congregation, and worshipers moved on to other churches. The landmark structure was renovated into professional offices, preserving the architectural beauty of the exterior and significantly changing the character of the interior. These changes didn't reduce the devotion of Daniel and Susannah to their beloved church, however. The ghosts of these spiritual leaders have been reported by Reverend Eduard Perry and several people who rent offices in the building.

The Reverend Bagley appears in a traditional black suit with stiff white collar. He has been seen standing on the stairs between the first and second floors, near the main entrance of the building, and in the bell tower. Those who have seen him report an eerie presence that precedes a partial or whole apparition. This ghost is not scary, but he catches people off guard because he looks so lifelike.

Susannah Bagley has been described as a floating apparition dressed in a long gown. A blue light surrounds her, making her appear angelic. Susannah also creates intense cold spots. It has been reported that this ghost spoke to a tenant of the building. She asked, "How do I get out?" The astonished tenant gave directions to the front entrance, but the ghost floated up the stairs and out a window.

This former church may be a good place to try EVP recordings. If Susannah has a tendency to speak to the living, she might like to leave a message on your audio recorder. Ghost haunters have picked up auditory phenomena on the first floor and in the former second-floor gallery that sounded like a blast of organ music and choir voices.

This building is now a private office complex called Catalysis, but access can be arranged by contacting the facility manager or speaking to the receptionist.

GHOSTS OF FEMINISTS

Harvard Exit Theatre
807 East Roy Street
Capitol Hill District
Seattle 98102-4610
206-323-8986

Passionate people in pursuit of passionate causes seldom give up, even after death. This may be the reason the Harvard Exit Theatre, built in the mid-1920s as headquarters for the Women's Century Club, is haunted by several ghosts.

The Women's Century Club was founded by many of Seattle's earliest feminists who fought for women's suffrage, equal rights on the job, and other causes. From its ranks, women rose to high positions in business, education, and politics, giving Seattle its first female mayor, Bertha Landes. A favorite gathering spot for club members was the sitting area near the fireplace on the first floor. Here, club leaders met to plan campaigns, argue strategy, and offer support to each other when their causes seemed to falter. This spot is still a gathering place for the Century Club, but some of the club members who show up now are ghosts.

Over the years, building managers have found the chairs rearranged for a meeting and even a fire blazing in the fireplace when they arrived for work in the morning. Visitors and people who work in the building have spotted many apparitions there. A frequent sighting is that of a woman seated in one of the chairs, dressed in a long, floral-print gown, with her hair gathered in a bun. This ghost appears lifelike and engrossed in a book she is reading. She acknowledges the presence of living beings by looking up from her book and smiling. After doing so, the ghost rises from her chair and walks out of the room. Another woman seen in this area turns light switches on and off and then vanishes. Ghost hunters who snap pictures of the fireplace sitting area have reportedly found transparent images of several women in their photographs. Orbs have been found, too.

On the second floor in the office area, a lifelike ghost has been found sobbing. When staff members move close to her to offer help, she vanishes. On the stairway leading to the second floor, visitors and staff have seen a woman hanging by a rope. This ghost may predate the Women's Century Club. Historical records reportedly indicate that a murder took place in a house that stood at the location. A male ghost, who appears at various locations in the building, sometimes causes trouble and may be linked to this crime. The man has been described as portly or rotund, dressed in mid-nineteenth-century clothing, and transparent. This fellow may be responsible for locking the projection-room door from the inside. One time, he locked the door, started the movie projector—for an invisible audience, for the theater was closed at the time—and moved film cans into a disorganized pile.

A recent manager, Alan Blangy, often sensed a hostile presence in the building and one night chased an unseen intruder through the deserted building to a fire-escape door. There, Blangy and the intruder fought a tug of war, with the manager trying to open the door. When the door finally flew open, no one was found on the fire escape at the side of the building thirty feet above the ground.

Ghost hunters who visit this popular movie theater should start by attending a scheduled screening of a movie. After getting a feel for the lobby—still decked out in 1920s décor—and other parts of the building accessible to theater customers, ghost hunters may detect a spot where a short vigil will result in a ghost sighting. A daytime visit may be arranged with the building manager for EVP, photography, and psychic investigation of the seating area. Historic photographs of Century Club members should be viewed first, especially that of Bertha Landes. These may be particularly useful in identifying a ghost or making contact with a spirit.

DAUGHTERS OF THE AMERICAN REVOLUTION RAINIER CHAPTER HOUSE

800 East Roy Street
Capitol Hill District
Seattle 98102-4611
206-323-0600

One look at this magnificent mansion and ghost hunters will think they've been mysteriously transported to Mount Vernon and dropped at the gate of George Washington's famous plantation. The white colonial building is, in fact, a replica of the first president's home and rightly serves as headquarters of the Rainier chapter of the Daughters of the American Revolution. The building is not generally open to the public, but access may be gained if you contact the facility manager in advance. The huge building is often booked for weddings, receptions, meetings, and special community social events.

According to www.theshadowlands.net, a Web site that chronicles ghostly activity, hauntings, and other mysterious events, the building was once a church, but this is not true. It was constructed in 1923 specifically for the DAR. Some church-related events have taken place there, but it is not a house of worship. The site also mentions reports of a female apparition walking down the stairs dressed in an 1800s-vintage gown. This report was probably inspired by DAR members who sometimes dress in gowns worn during the presidency of George Washington. In fact, near the main staircase, a framed picture hangs on the wall showing some of the ladies enjoying tea in the main pallor while decked out in early American fashions.

Upstairs, though, ghost hunters may run into paranormal phenomena that may indicate the presence of a ghost. On the second floor, the ballroom stretches nearly the length of the house. Dark stained floors, a small stage at one end, and bright white walls make the room look like anything but the stereotypical haunted mansion. But when I visited in November 2005, I detected intense, isolated cold cells moving slowly around the ballroom floor. The movement of these cold cells

The headquarters of Daughters of the American Revolution Rainier chapter, a replica of George Washington's Mount Vernon estate, may be home to spirits from the 1920s.

resembled the movement of dancers as they waltzed counterclockwise to unheard music. Digital images failed to capture orbs or any other environmental anomaly that are often linked to cold cells.

The ballroom of the DAR chapter house would be a good venue for attempts at EVP and thermography. With a history of parties, social events, and meetings that dates from 1923, it is most certain environmental imprints have been created there.

EGYPTIAN THEATRE

805 East Pine Street
Capitol Hill District
Seattle 98122-3837
206-323-4978

The first theater in Seattle called the Egyptian opened in the University district. It stayed in business as a second-run movie house for many years before its fixtures, projection equipment, security features, and seating fell irreparably behind the times. That building was renovated in the late 1960s and reopened as a drugstore. The Egyptian Theatre on East Pine Street is the third to have the name. It is the second incarnation of a dream held by two Canadians, Darrel MacDonald and Dan Ireland.

In 1975, MacDonald and Ireland remodeled the old Moore Theatre in downtown Seattle with Egyptian architectural features and color motif. They were completely enamored with Egyptian art and believed that theaters were sufficiently large enough structures to serve as a showplace for the ancient styles of sculpture, fabrics, architectural features, and even plants. The Moore was reopened in 1975 as the Moore Egyptian Theatre. After a short run of only five years, MacDonald and Ireland lost their lease and were forced to find another location. They found this six-hundred-seat Masonic auditorium in the Capitol Hill district and went to work transforming it into yet another tribute to Egyptian art and architecture. The theater now thrives and serves as the permanent home of the Seattle International Film Festival.

Like most theaters, the Egyptian has a ghost. The fellow who roams the aisles of this movie house, however, may be left over from the days when the building was a Masonic temple. The ghost of the Egyptian Theatre appears dark and billowing and roughly the shape of a human. Witnesses describe this ghost as large, rotund, and lacking in detail. No one has seen his face, hands, arms, or even legs. He appears as though he is wearing a hooded cloak that falls to his ankles.

This fellow drifts up and down the aisles at the end of the midnight movie on Friday and Saturday nights. He doesn't try to get the attention of patrons or theater staff members, but he has left a lot of people stunned and even shocked. He is seen when the house lights come up and tired patrons are getting ready to leave their seats.

When this building served as a Masonic temple, many secret rituals were conducted there, some with cloaks, capes, large hats, and even hoods. This ghost likely died during a meeting of his fellow Masons, perhaps dressed in full Masonic regalia. Ghosts associated with theaters usually hang out in dressing rooms, backstage areas, or projection booths.

Other places to hunt ghosts in central Seattle:

Cherry Street Coffee House

2721 First Avenue
Seattle 98121-1101
206-441-5489

This building used to house the city morgue. Over the years several businesses tried to make a go of it—a steak house, a French bistro, a Thai restaurant, and most recently, the upscale Avenue One—but they all failed in a short time. Sometimes, this means a building harbors a ghost or two that object to the building or business that occupies the space.

Josephinum Apartments

1902 Second Avenue
Seattle 98101-1155
206-448-8500

This building started out as the upscale New Washington Hotel in 1908. A little historical research reveals that it was constructed on ground that was the city's first cemetery. The fourteenth floor, which is operated by the Catholic Church as apartments for the elderly, is haunted. Several spirits have been spotted walking the hallways and sitting on the stairs. Check out the magnificent marble paneling, balustrades, and arches in the lobby. To the left of the lobby, the former hotel dining room now serves as a chapel.

The Baltic Room

1207 Pine Street
Seattle 98101
206-625-4444

At least three ghosts have been seen there—two females and one male. One couple may have been former owners of this popular Capitol Hill night spot. All three have been seen as partial apparitions. One of the women appears in a calf-length skirt that swishes when she walks.

The Rendezvous Lounge

2320 Second Avenue
Seattle 98121
206-441-5823

This Belltown watering hole was a speakeasy during Prohibition. During the 1940s, the building was used as a movie theater. A small room, used as the projection booth, is home to a ghost. This spirit is probably the projectionist who loves movies so much that he can't leave the place, even after his death. There are reports of a swarthy-looking fellow floating about the place. He may have been a gambler or card dealer during the 1920s.

CHAPTER 5

University District and North Seattle

The University of Washington campus and its surrounding community are only a short drive from central Seattle. Across Lake Union and the
Portage Bay Channel, a charming neighborhood surrounds the campus
with old theaters, shops, cafés, and bars, many of which are said to be
haunted. On campus, the four fascinating columns that stand at the head
of the amphitheater are the only remnants of the original university building that once stood in central Seattle. They are haunted by the professor
who saved them from destruction. Beyond the campus, places such as the
College Inn Pub, Green Lake, and Good Shepherd Center offer ghost
hunters a glimpse of old Seattle and a chance to encounter ghosts.

THE LADY IN GRAY

Neptune Theatre
1303 Forty-Fifth Street Northeast (at Thirteenth Avenue)
University District
Seattle 98105-5808
206-632-3131

The Neptune is the perfect name for this movie house located in
the University District. The 1940s-era marquee lights up the street
with the titles of classic Hollywood films, independent films, and for-
eign-language cinema. The theater opened in 1940 as the Neptune
and has survived big changes in movie-projection technology, customer demands, and renovations.

The female ghost that haunts this charming movie house does not seem to be linked to the theater business or movies. Her apparition, with dark brown hair and a long gray gown, appears to float across the lobby floor oblivious to evening crowds or staff performing after-hours maintenance. Some witnesses have spotted her in the lady's restroom. Her torso appears in the mirror, and astonished patrons have nearly fainted at the sight of this transparent ghost. Using psychic methods of investigation, no explanation has been found for this ghost of the lady in gray. It is likely she occupied the site before the theater was built.

There may be other ghosts in the Neptune Theatre. Reports indicate that theater painter Jeff Kurtii has experienced the presence of an unseen entity as it rushed past him. This entity was definitely not female. In fact, ghost hunters say the ghost is often accompanied by the odor of burning tobacco, so he's been called the Smoking Ghost. Theater regulars say the odor of burning tobacco is fairly common in the old movie house. Sitting in one of the comfortable seats at the rear of the screening room, it is common to feel as though someone is sitting right behind you. A glance around, however, reveals nothing but empty seats.

THE WATER GHOST

Wells Fargo Bank
Forty-Fifth Street at University Way Northeast
University District
Seattle 98105
206-547-2811

This federal-style bank building poses a challenge to ghost hunters because it is a place where security is a serious matter. The historic bank serves its customers well, but it is not in the business of hosting paranormal investigations. If a ghost hunter finds the building fascinating and the haunting intriguing, a formal request must be made to the manager before ghost hunting can take place. If permission is obtained, ghost hunters may have an interesting experience in the lower floor of this bank.

Several reports describe a tall, masculine shadow, without discernible facial features, that wanders the lower floor of the bank. The specter turns lights on and off, but more often expends his energy manipulating water. If a cup of water is left on a desk, he tips it. If a faucet is not tightly shut, he opens it. Water bottles brought in by employees may disappear from bags only to turn up several feet away in odd places. This ghost also creates the sound of running water when no faucets are open. The sound seems to come from restrooms and overhead water pipes. An explanation for this ghostly manifestation may be found in historical descriptions of the land dating from the 1880s.

The Wells Fargo Bank, at Forty-Fifth Street and University Way, was constructed on land once occupied by the Brownsfield farm. When developer James Moore surveyed the land and neighboring farms for a proposed an extension of the city of Seattle—and site of a major university nearby—he noted a large frog pond at the place where his proposed University Way and Forty-Fifth Street would intersect. Nearby, a stream ran full, supplying the Brownsfield farm with fresh water. After Moore's streets were laid out, the stream caused some erosion, so conduits were installed to alter its course and a trestle was built over it to support a trolley track. As the area developed and larger buildings were constructed—such as Wells Fargo Bank—regrading was done, and the frog pond disappeared. The stream, however, persisted and posed a problem for builders. Eventually, an underground water course was devised. Remnants of the stream can still be seen by accessing the underground course via a trap door in the lower floor of the bank.

The presence of this persistent stream may account for the affinity of the bank's ghost for water. San Diego-based ghost hunter and author John Lamb has suggested that natural water may increase the vigor and frequency of a haunting. In fact, some paranormal investigators look for unknown springs, hidden wells, and filled ponds when they search a site for the source of hauntings or other bizarre phenomena. Spirits may use water as a means of modulating their vibration frequency so they may manifest on our plane of existence.

PHANTOMS OF THE FOUR COLUMNS

Sylvan Theater and the Great Columns
Pine Avenue at Boren Street
University of Washington
206-598-6647

One of the ghosts seen near the historic columns of the University of Washington's Sylvan Theater may be that of Professor Edmond Meany, the man who saved them from demolition in 1910.

At the Sylvan Theater—also known as the Columns—visitors feel a foreboding, uneasy atmosphere, especially at night. The entity that haunts this place reportedly growls, shakes shrubs and trees, and creates odd vibrations as if this unseen being is stomping its feet on the ground. People come away with the impression that the ghost is angry and dislikes visitors. Those who have seen the entity say it appears to be a young male dressed in dark clothing with a translucent scarf wrapped around his neck. There is no other information about this entity, but ghost hunters believe he moved to the site with the four columns when they were relocated from the old university campus downtown. The angry ghost may have been expelled from the institution or maybe failed his classes.

Another entity detected at this location is much less active but welcomes visitors with a congenial presence. He seems happy that people are paying attention to the four columns that stand across the earthen stage of the amphitheater. Often, visitors feel him stand close by or the sensation of a warm hand on their shoulder even on the coldest days.

The four columns have an interesting history that points to the identity of at least one of the entities attached to them. The original University of Washington building was erected at Fourth Street and University Avenue in downtown Seattle in the 1860s. Four twenty-four-foot cedar columns marked its main entrance, giving the otherwise plain building classic features that appealed to academics. By 1895, the student population outgrew the building, so a new campus was constructed north of the city on Union Bay. The original university building was rented as offices and anchored a new business district called the Metropolitan Tract.

By 1910, the old building had deteriorated so badly that it was scheduled for demolition. Professor Edmond Meany, head of the history department and one of the university's first graduates, implored alumni and friends of the university to preserve its birthplace by dismantling the building and reassembling it on the new campus. But the fund-raising effort fell short of its goal, and Meany only had enough support to spare the stately columns and relocate them to a parklike setting at the edge of the new campus. Meany lamented that people were more interested in making money than spending it to foster "the sentiment or regard for an old building. In the years to come there are sure to be many regrets."

After relocation of the four columns, the grounds surrounding them were developed into an amphitheater where graduation ceremonies, plays, banquets, and weddings were staged. Edmond Meany became the unofficial guardian of the columns and demonstrated his attachment to them by naming them Loyalty, Industry, Faith, and Efficiency. The first letters of these names formed the acronym LIFE. The columns have now withstood more than ninety years of exposure to the region's climate, reminding students, faculty, and visitors of the early days of the university.

With such a strong attachment to the four columns, it seems likely that the benevolent entity who haunts them is the ghost of Professor Edmond Meany. His acronym for the four columns may be a clue that his spirit lives on at this special place.

Located a few feet behind the western-most column, among the shrubs, is a monument to Professor Meany donated by the class of 1885. A large stone serves as the base for a bronze medallion featuring a likeness of Edmond Meany and the words "In Memoriam."

VOICES AND HEAVY BOOTS

University YMCA
5003 Twelfth Avenue Northeast
University District
Seattle 98105-4306
206-524-1400

This busy community center doesn't look haunted. People come and go constantly, most spending an hour or so exercising or taking a class. Kids run around a bit, the place is well lit, and there aren't any secret rooms or locked attics where ghosts might lurk. But members of AGHOST list this YMCA as a haunted place.

In the early 1990s, cleaning staff working in the basement exercise room reported hearing voices coming from the floor above. These experiences became more frequent and occurred at times when no one was working after hours on the main floor. Many times, two sets of heavy footsteps were heard, as if two people were walking away from each other in opposite directions.

By 1993, the voices and footsteps were more intense and frequent, and YMCA members exercising in the evening mentioned them to the lone staff member who worked on the floor above. They became noteworthy because the voices sometimes argued or sounded as though someone were in distress.

Investigations by local ghost hunters identified a presence in the furnace room but did not turn up clues as to the identity of the entities that created the disembodied voices or footsteps. Yet, an online search turns up old maps and photographs of the district before it was developed as a university community. The material reveals a logging camp and several farms scattered across this area. Ghosts who tread the floor of the YCMA in heavy boots were possibly lumberjacks who cleared the land in the 1870s. Some may have been farmers of the 1880s, road builders of the 1890s, or construction workers who built the YMCA in the 1960s.

GHOST OF SYLVIA GAINES

Green Lake Park
5701 East Green Lake Drive at Aurora Avenue North
Seattle 98115
206-985-9235

Northwest from the University District is an urban oasis called Green Lake. Covering more than ten acres, the placid water anchors the surrounding community with a peaceful ambience and cool breezes. Playgrounds, swimming areas, boating, food concessions, walking and jogging trails, and a small theater provide numerous opportunities for locals to get outdoors and commune with nature.

Sites along the lakeshore offer visitors a chance to commune with the dead, too. At the swimming area on the west side of the lake, ghosts of drowning victims have been spotted in broad daylight. Astonished walkers, joggers, and bikers have seen swimmers waving frantically as they bob at the surface midway between the dock and the beach. Stopping in midstride, these people take a second look only to see no one there. For decades, reports of swimmers in jeopardy were made to lifeguards, lake supervisors, and police, but no victims were found or reported missing. It is believed that these ghost swimmers drowned many years ago when Green Lake was an out-of-town destination for Seattle residents looking for exercise or recreation. Throughout the 1920s, '30s, and '40s, several swimmers, sailors, and kayakers drowned in this lake. Due to heavy growth of algae and other organic debris, many of these victims were never recovered.

The most famous ghost of Green Lake did not lose her life in a swimming or boating accident. Twenty-five-year-old Sylvia Gaines was murdered along the north shore on June 17, 1926. Her body was dragged to a location near a walking path in a grove of cottonwoods (recently replaced with poplars) and staged to look like she had been assaulted and raped on the spot, then murdered by strangulation.

This tragedy alarmed the surrounding community and led to the discovery of an unlikely perpetrator. Sylvia was born in Massachusetts in 1904. Her father, Bob Gaines, divorced her mother when she was five and moved to Seattle. More than twenty years latter, Sylvia traveled west to reunite with her father. According to accounts by Bob's

The ghost of murder victim Sylvia Gaines still wanders the shore of Green Lake.

second wife and others, Sylvia moved into her father's house at 108 North Fifty-First Street, and the two acted more like lovers than father and daughter. In fact, the couple was observed together in bed, parked on lover's lane, and engaged in fierce arguments over their housing arrangement, which included Bob's second wife.

When Sylvia's body was found, a tearful Bob Gaines identified the remains and remarked that some creep from the neighborhood must have killed his sweet daughter. Later, he admitted to having an argument with his daughter earlier in the evening on June 17, after which she stormed out the house and walked toward the lake. As investigators uncovered the incestuous relationship, Bob became the prime suspect. In spite of no physical evidence, he was tried and convicted of first-degree murder and hanged.

Sylvia's ghost still wanders the north-shore area named Gaines Point. Psychics have not discovered the reason for her presence, but some suspect that Sylvia is looking for her true murderer. Also, she may be waiting for her father to find her and take her home. The woman's pale apparition hides behind the trees and shrubs, revealing only part of her face. She behaves as if she is afraid to leave her hiding place. This frail ghost has been spotted in daylight, but most sightings occur after sunset.

Bob Gaines was convicted with circumstantial evidence that included hearsay from a drinking buddy who was rarely sober. If Bob and Sylvia had not engaged in incest, it is likely that the jury would have looked more favorably on the man and he would have been acquitted. Some ghost hunters have wondered if Bob's ghost is also wandering the north shore of Green Lake seeking to reunite with his daughter.

GHOST OF THE GOOD SISTERS AND SALVAGED CHILDREN

Good Shepherd Center
4649 Sunnyside Avenue North
Seattle 98103-6900
206-547-8127 (Property Manager's Office)

This huge brick building was designed by architect Alfred C. Breitung and opened as a home for girls in 1907. The Sisters of the Good Shepherd ran the institution known as the Home of the Good Shepherd. They offered safety, a few comforts, an education, and vocational training to orphaned or delinquent girls.

The Home of the Good Shepherd was a strict place where girls learned to follow the rules or suffer severe consequences at the hands of the nuns. The north wing housed "good" girls who were most often orphans. The south wing housed the "penitent" girls. Rising at dawn, the girls worked in the kitchens, laundry, fruit orchard, and at other necessary tasks before school started. After school, the nuns provided music lessons for the girls with a little talent, while others took classes in typing, sewing, or choir. Visitors were not allowed except for a few hours on Sunday afternoons under the supervision of chaperones. The girls were not permitted to leave the campus until the rules were relaxed in the 1970s. Accounts published on the Web along with several historic photographs, describe the Home of the

The Good Shepherd Center was a refuge for orphaned girls. The ghosts of some of them may still roam the hallways.

Good Shepherd as a life-saving institution in spite of the strict rules. A few years there doubtless saved many girls from miserable lives among the dregs of society. By the early 1970s, various government-supported social services made the home obsolete. The Good Shepherd Center closed its doors in June 1973, after sixty-five years of strict daily routines under the watchful eyes of nuns swift to punish but quick to offer a loving hand.

Today, the stunning building and its thirteen-acre grounds are known as the Sunnyside Center. It is owned and operated by Historic Seattle and houses the Meridian School, the Neo Art School, the Wallingford Senior Center, and several nonprofit organizations. In spite of the changes, many tenants and visitors often catch a glimpse of a nun's habit swishing around a corner or hear the quiet chatter of girls as they walk double file to class.

Ghostly visions and sounds are common experiences there. Ghost hunters have found an eerie presence on each of the five floors. The paranormal activity is probably an environmental imprint triggered by, or revealed to, sensitive people. The strict daily routine, carried out year after year by frightened girls who lost their parents or suffered abuse at home, would leave an impression at several places such as the former dining hall, laundry room, and wide stairs. The nuns also left their marks on the environment. Apparitions of a nun's habit have been spotted at several places including the garden.

There are no records of deaths at the Home of the Good Shepherd, but it is likely some of the nuns passed away there. Even if death caught up to a nun living elsewhere, her spirit might have returned to a place where her life was given to the service of others.

The most dramatic event to occur at the Good Shepherd Center was a fire that raged through the fifth floor on August 7, 1967. A resident, entrusted with the key to a storage room, started the blaze that nearly destroyed the south wing of the attic. Fortunately, no deaths resulted from this tragedy. Today, this floor has an eerie presence with cold spots and a thickened atmosphere.

CELL OF FEAR AND VOICES FROM THE FOREST

Nathan Hale High School
10750 Thirtieth Avenue
Kenmore 98125
206-252-3680

This flashy, steel and glass high school doesn't look like the kind of place that would be haunted. Bright sunlight penetrates the modern buildings through floor-to-ceiling windows, eliminating any chance of a musty atmosphere or ghostly shadows. The story associated with this public high school is that a girl was raped in one of the hallways. A search of local newspaper archives failed to turn up any reliable information about such a tragic event. If no fatality occurred, the crime probably received little press so as not to alarm other students and their families. The paranormal phenomena reported there includes odd noises—possibly sounds of distress—and a localized cold area or cell in one of the hallways. Some say that when sensitive people walk through this cell, they become frightened, as if some unseen threat has closed around them.

This report sounds like a haunting rather than the presence of the ghost of a rape victim. A haunting is a residual environmental imprint created by a strong emotion or intense energy associated with an unusual event. Events that create imprints include rapes, muggings, fights, shootings, serious accidents such as falling down stairs, and death. The paranormal phenomenon experienced may be an odor, sound, partial apparition of a human form, unusual lights or shadows, cold spots, intense electromagnetic-field aberrations, or other environmental anomalies. Sensitive people may become aware of sudden, inexplicable emotions such as fear, rage, or hate. The cell of fear, reported by several people who have walked the hallway at this high school, may indicate the site where a rape or some equally devastating event took place.

The law requires visitors to a public school to register at the office and obtain a pass before roaming the campus. Ghost hunters should call a few days ahead of a visit to obtain permission for a brief tour after students have left the building.

If planning ahead is not an option, there is another haunted site on this campus that is accessible to the public without a pass. At the south border of the campus, between the baseball fields and Northeast 150th Street, is a forested area, the site of unexplained voices and lights. Residents who live on this street facing the forested area told me that a knife fight took place amid the trees many years ago. Now, at least a few times each month, strange dots of light are seen in the trees at night as sharp screams ring out. People have crossed the street several times to investigate, thinking another fight has occurred only to find the area vacant. Most of this paranormal activity occurs in the trees separating the middle and eastern-most baseball fields.

WEIRD STUFF

Saint Edwards State Park and Bastyr University
14445 Juanita Drive
Kenmore 98028
425-823-1300

This heavily forested state park surrounds the campus of Bastyr University. Founded in 1978, the university offers graduate and undergraduate degrees in naturopathic medicine, acupuncture, Oriental medicine, nutrition, exercise science, herbal sciences, and several other natural-health programs. With more than 1,200 students and a large faculty focused on nontraditional health practices, a visitor might expect to find a different academic atmosphere. The university offers several traditional and demanding science courses and study tracts, but there is something peculiar about the place. The dense forests make you feel that something lurks in the darkness, just beyond your vision. At several spots near the ball fields and in the herb garden, sensitive people feel atmosphere anomalies created by strong electromagnetic fields.

Ghost hunters have reported the sounds of disembodied children running around the playground. Some ghost hunters have captured EVP on their audio recorders. In visiting the site at night, ghost hunters have found orbs on their photographs. How these ghost children got there is still a mystery. One theory is that they are spirit remnants from an Indian village that once occupied the site. These grounds, located on the eastern shore of Lake Washington, are recognized as Indian habitats.

Inside some of Bastyr University's buildings, weird things happen. A member of the faculty, who insisted on anonymity, described ceiling-mounted light fixtures that swayed for no apparent reason. He also told of cold spots and chairs that slide around on the linoleum floors. Most of the weird stuff described by this faculty member occurs in a basement classroom and in a first-floor conference room. With a history that dates back to 1978, there is no tragic event, such as a fire or other disaster that might have led to a haunting.

Research into the history of this location revealed that the 316 acres occupied by the state park and university were purchased by the Diocese of Seattle in 1920 for use as a seminary for the Society of Saint-Sulpice. The order constructed St. Edward Seminary in 1931, but sold the buildings and part of the land to Bastyr University in 1977. This accounts for the ecclesiastical appearance of some of the university's facilities. During the forty-six years the seminary occupied the campus, it is likely that some deaths occurred, some of them sudden or accidental. The spirits of the deceased, devoted to the order, may still roam the rooms where they lived and studied.

It is possible that Indian spirits or long-dead pioneers who homesteaded the property might be snooping around to see what has become of their cherished grounds. Ghost hunters should also consider the possibility of poltergeist activity attributable to a disturbed, living person.

GHOST IN THE GIRLS' BATHROOM

Hamilton Middle School
1610 North Forty-First Street
Seattle 98103
206-252-5810

This four-story brick building houses a well-respected middle school. Looking more like a high school, the imposing structure towers over the surrounding community of modest homes. The building dates from the 1940s, and in spite of the school's modern curriculum and unique programs, the building has retained an old atmosphere. Fixtures throughout the building remind visitors of the school's vintage and conjure up notions of spirits left over from past decades. As a reminder, visitors must check in at the school's office before wandering around.

Like most schools of this era, Hamilton Middle School is said to be haunted. In fact, the story most widely told is similar to stories told at many schools throughout the country. A student got pregnant on or nearby the school's grounds, and she later died in the second-floor girls' bathroom. Most stories of this kind include a student's death, usually as a result of a fight or suicide. Ghost hunters can easily be led astray by these urban myths that are most often told by older students to frighten newcomers. The reports posted for this location include bizarre sightings in the girls' second-floor bathroom. Vague shapes resembling a young female appear in the mirror, and doors open and close by unseen hands.

There is no public information about the death of a female student at Hamilton Middle School. In the fall of 2005, I interviewed a man who had worked for many years at the school as a janitor. He was familiar with the story outlined above but added that there are other strange things that happen at the school. The janitor, who requested anonymity, said that many doors throughout the school open and close on their own. This usually occurs in the evening after students and faculty have gone. If the door is locked, the door handle or panic bar shakes as if someone is trying to open the door from the other side. Many times he has pushed the door open, expecting to find a late-working teacher, but found no one there.

As for the haunting of the second-floor girls' bathroom, the janitor said a plumber died in the room during construction of the school. The unfortunate fellow was working alone and suffered a fatal heart attack. He was not discovered until the end of the shift, when it was too late to save him. In spite of upgrades done in the room over the years, janitorial staff always feel odd sensations when they enter the room. When asked about the mirror, he said that it breaks often, as many as three times a year, while other mirrors in the building have lasted for decades.

COLLEGE INN PUB

4006 University Way Northeast
Seattle 98105
206-634-2307

Drinking establishments located near universities are often haunted.

This is especially true if the watering hole is housed in an old building that has seen generations of students and faculty struggle through some of the most demanding yet exhilarating years of their lives. Students may spend about four or five years at a favorite bar close to campus, but faculty may show up for decades, especially if they have tenure. At the College Inn Pub near the University of Washington, ghosts of students and faculty have been seen, unable to pull themselves away from a favorite booth or barstool and the academic camaraderie that cannot be found anywhere else.

Aside from a transition from life to death that may have occurred at college bars, ghosts may be attracted to and held at these places because the bars were the only places in life where they felt comfortable—both in an academic and social sense. Also, friends could also be counted on to show up on a regular basis. Ghosts who haunt college bars may be hanging around for a challenging game of chess, a rousing academic debate with drinking buddies, a game of pool, or the aroma of good food and the taste of a favorite brew. The College Inn Pub offers these in fine style to the living and the dead.

Aside from proximity to campus and a fascinating clientele, the pub is housed in a historic building. Looking a bit like a Swiss chalet, with gables, peaked roofs, and decorated façades, the building was constructed in 1908 as housing for visitors attending the Alaska-Yukon-Pacific Exposition of 1909. After the exposition, the upper floors were remodeled as a hotel to serve the business district that grew rapidly at the edge of the campus. Years later, the basement was enlarged and opened as a pub. Today, visitors may stay at the College Inn and search for ghosts in some of the rooms or descend the staircase from the back alley to the pub.

The pub has been described as subterranean and turretlike. In fact, the sprawling, dimly lit rooms make visitors feel like they've descended into the bowels of the earth. The pub is divided into three areas. One area has a couple pool tables. Another, anchored by the bar, contains several booths. The booths are in the darker of the two spaces, comfortable and cozy, featuring some interesting graffiti on the table tops. Owner Rich Burnett described the third space as the snug room. It is partitioned from the other spaces by glass

In the basement pub of this historic building, ghosts of students and faculty still linger over drinks.

walls that create a room for private parties and meetings. The snug room has an upright piano that has been known to play Irish tunes without a visible musician seated on the bench. Even if the keys don't appear to move, sensitive people hear the muted notes from the old piano.

The partial apparition of an Irish fellow has been seen in the booth area drinking beer. This ghost moves glasses around on the tables, and many observers suspect he finishes their drinks while they make a quick trip to the restroom. Many people have also seen the apparition of an older man, described as a codger, at the bar. This ghost wears a trench coat and a deerstalker hat, Sherlock Holmes style. Some astonished witnesses report that the man's coat appears wet, as if he has just stepped in from the rain.

People who use the restrooms sometimes report disembodied voices heard there. Ghost hunters should be aware that this is not a paranormal experience. The acoustics of this old place allow barroom chatter to penetrate the walls of the restrooms and vice versa. However, some have detected intense cold spots in the men's restroom, no doubt the site where many young college men have suffered wretched vomiting and near-death experiences.

CHAPTER 6

Communities North of Seattle

Ghost hunters looking for an exciting day trip or weekend beyond central Seattle should head north. Historic towns along the ninety-mile stretch from Seattle to Bellingham have plenty of haunted buildings and beautiful scenery. The historic district of Fairhaven is a worthwhile destination that offers several haunted places within blocks of each other. A more exotic destination, reached by hopping on a seaplane or ferryboat, is the San Juan Islands. Amazing vistas, closeups with orcas, and some fascinating haunted places can easily fill a weekend.

GHOST OF THE EDMONDS THEATER

415 Main Street
Edmonds 98020
425-778-4554

Old theaters have a charm all their own. Some of that comes from elegant architecture, a history that includes performances by famous people, or an atmosphere laced with the passion of actors, musicians, and directors. The charm of the Edmonds Theater also includes something ghostly.

The theater that anchors the historic district of Edmonds was built in 1923. A retired dentist, Jacques Mayo, ran the theater from 1960 until 1989. At first, the theater was called The Princess, then the Edgemont, and finally, in 1989, it became the Edmonds Theater. The glass-paneled double doors are original, but they open to a

The ghost of former owner Jacques Mayo watches over the quaint Edmonds Theater.

lobby that has been rebuilt a number of times. The lobby seems much larger thanks to a mirror that rises from floor to ceiling. I learned that theater staff members and patrons often see a shadowy figure in this mirror, but when they turn to look for it, it is not standing in the lobby.

There are other reports that a glowing apparition has been spotted floating the aisles late at night as the last patrons leave the 252-seat theater. Some believe this is the ghost of former owner Jacques Mayo. Given the long history of the theater, is it likely that at least one patron died in the house. His spirit may still be looking for an exit. In the 1920s and '30s, theaters such as this often showed film all night, as homeless patrons dozed in the seats after coughing up twenty cents for admission. Two dimes could not buy a room, but it allowed entry to a warm and dry theater that also offered a restroom.

Today the Edmonds Theater has an updated sound system and a

comfortable balcony, and it shows first-run movies. But its historic charms remain, enjoyed by the living and the dead.

GHOST OF THE DEDICATED TEACHER

Frances E. Anderson Cultural and Leisure Center
700 Main Street
Edmonds 98020
425-771-0230

This busy community center is haunted by the ghost of Frances E. Anderson, but there may be other spirits roaming the hallways as well. The center occupies a building that was constructed in 1929 and served as the Edmonds Elementary School for nearly fifty years. Anderson taught at this school for many years before becoming its last principal. When the facility was renovated and reopened as a community center, the townspeople named the place in her honor. Today, the Anderson Center houses several organizations that offer classes in cultural arts, fitness, martial arts, and ballet, as well as recreational programs, a day-care center, and a youth club.

The ghost of Frances Anderson has been seen walking the hallways and descending the flight of stairs that stand to the right of the long hall. She appears as a partial apparition with shoulders, arms, and head and is said to look pleased with all the activity at her former school.

Several people have reported the sound of children in the hallways when the place is nearly deserted. Current tenants in the building told me about the sound of several children talking and laughing as the invisible group moved down the main-floor corridor. A similar experience has occurred in halls of the upper floors. This kind of paranormal activity is probably a haunting—an environmental imprint of a past event that does not indicate the presence of a spirit of a dead person. Others have suggested that spirits of the dead may have gravitated back to the place they were most happy in life—their school.

In addition to Frances Anderson, the ghost of a deceased teacher is believed to haunt the second floor. People who have been on the floor alone before the building opens for classes have heard an unseen presence say, "Good morning."

GHOST OF THE THEATER PATRON

The New Everett Theatre
2911 Colby Avenue
Everett 98201
425-258-6766

When the Everett Theatre opened in 1901, its 1,200 seats could accommodate one-sixth of the town's residents. Aside from movies, the Everett Theatre was one of only three in the area equipped for live performances. In fact, some of the greatest stage performers of the 1920s and '30s appeared there, including Al Jolson, Lillian Russell, Helen Hayes, George M. Cohan, and Eddie Foy and the Seven Little Foys. The interior of this entertainment palace was as fancy as any that could be found in Seattle or Portland, but most of its patrons were loggers, fishermen, or farmers.

In 1923, the Everett Theatre was nearly destroyed by fire, but it was quickly rebuilt at a cost of $250,000. It underwent another rebuild in 1952 with the hope that its performances could compete with television. Two additional movie screens were added in 1979, but attendance declined until 1989, when the building was closed. Concerned citizens formed the Everett Theatre Society. They preserved and restored this gem, opening its doors for special events and performances, meetings, parties, and fundraisers. Throughout these many changes, a mysterious presence has remained on the premises expressing an interest in the people and the things they are doing to this beloved theater.

For nearly thirty years, patrons, theater staff members, and renovators have reported encounters with an elderly male presence. Many have gotten the impression that this ghost is a devoted patron or a former employee. Psychic investigations of the site have confirmed the presence of a spirit. The entity has been located in the balcony, the aisles of the main floor, backstage, and in the lobby near the four white columns.

Theaters seem to be magnets for ghosts because of the energy emitted by the creative passion of performers, production staff, musicians, and others who create spectacular moments. There is something about this process that holds theater staff to these sites after death. Also, the allure of performers captures the fascination of patrons and keeps them coming back to see a favorite actor or actress, even if the patrons have been dead many years.

THE GHOST OF THE TAXI DRIVER

Mallard Cove Apartments
12402 Admiralty Way, Building G
Everett 98204
425-353-1100

Residents in Building G of this large, modern apartment complex tell of finding notes next to their telephones scribbled in a style that is not their own. The notes are often nothing more than an address and a time. Sometimes a cross street is included. The truly freaky thing about this is that the person who makes these notes enters and leaves apartments without signs of forcible entry. Even stranger, the mysterious note writer opens doors that are locked with a dead bolt and then leaves them open.

This weird phenomenon went on for quite awhile before residents began talking among themselves, comparing experiences and linking the odd notes to the apparition of a man that was often seen in the hallways of the three-story building. A caretaker at the apartment complex offered me a bit of information about a taxi driver named Bill Stein, which brought everything into focus.

In 1999, taxi driver Bill Stein turned off busy Admiralty Way into the peaceful grounds of the Mallard Cove Apartments. He came to a stop in front of Building G to drop off his customer, a middle-age woman. While helping the woman carry her luggage to the second floor, Stein began to experience chest pains and shortness of breath. Sweating profusely and feeling dizzy, he made his way back to his cab and dropped into the driver's seat. Before he could start the engine or pick up his radio to call for help, he died of a heart attack.

The ghost of Bill Stein is believed to be the mysterious note writer of Building G. The brief notes he makes—the address of his next customer—are typical of those made by drivers. Apparently, Stein enters Building G apartments, uses the phone, and often leaves the doors open. Some residents of the apartments claim to have seen Stein. They describe him as a man in his late forties wearing sweat pants, a T-shirt, and a Mariners baseball hat.

Building G is accessible to visitors, but ghost hunters should pay a courtesy call to the complex manager before roaming around. Some of the residents of Building G speak freely about the ghost of Bill Stein; some may even share the ghostly notes he has left behind. Others refuse to say a word.

GHOST OF THE JANITOR ON DUTY

Everett Inn
12619 Fourth Avenue
Everett 98204
425-347-9099 or 800-434-9204

By all appearances, this place is a modern, busy hotel without a hint of a bizarre past, hidden mystery, or unscrupulous business that might have resulted in a haunting. Located near busy 128th Street Southwest and Interstate 5, the inn is filled with people coming and going throughout the day and evening, leaving little opportunity for a quiet atmosphere in the lobby, hallways, or other spaces where a ghost might be found. But this nice hotel is haunted. One employee, who I interviewed in May 2006 and who requested to remain anonymous, said that ghostly activity described on www.theshadowlands.net is true.

Although the building has been standing for less than twenty years, a ghost roams about the basement. No one knows why he is there. There is no record of a staff member dying on the premises or even a serious accident. The ghost who haunts the basement is dressed in a janitor's uniform. On surveillance cameras, his clothing appears gray. Those who have seen this ghost say his pants and shirt are blue. Apparently, this man has been seen many times on the closed-circuit security system, but no one has made a recording of the images. The best guess is that this ghost used to work at the hotel, but died elsewhere. Devoted to his job, he still shows up, in uniform, and putters around the basement.

This ghost is a noisy one, but unlike poltergeists he is not disruptive or destructive. He slams the doors of washers and dryers, creating loud noises. Witnesses, who have gone down to the basement to investigate, report the sounds of tools and other metal objects being dropped on the concrete floor, as well as sneezing and the shuffling of heavy boots over the floor.

Someone posted a story on the Internet that describes a little girl who bypassed the elevator's lock and descended to the basement. There, she encountered the ghost and was actually observed on the security television talking to an invisible entity. Security staff scrambled to the basement after they heard a muffled male voice responding to the girl. When they arrived to retrieve her, they found the girl standing alone and no other person in the basement.

It is interesting to note that the hotel has changed hands twice. Businesses that fail after a short time or have frequent changes in ownership may harbor something paranormal.

GHOST OF THE GRAND PATRON

Mount Baker Theatre
104 North Commercial Street
Bellingham 98225
360-733-5793
www.mountbakertheatre.com

The Mount Baker Theatre is a Pacific Northwest jewel. Opened on April 29, 1927, the formidable stage and movie house was part of a nationwide movement to establish theaters of monumental proportions in the hearts of American cities. Following film mogul William Fox's directive, architect R. C. Reamer constructed a movie palace with grand artistic features in a Moorish-Spanish motif. Reamer also used imaginative construction techniques that have enabled the building to stand more than eighty years without structural problems. The sprawling building fills a city block, and its cupola-capped tower is visible from many points in Bellingham. Inside, the theater resembles the palace envisioned by William Fox. A huge light fixture nearly spans the ceiling of the 130-foot-by-250-foot auditorium. As visitors enter the huge lobby, a faux wood ceiling with decorated beams—in traditional Moorish style—rises to the spacious mezzanine that stands behind five columns connected with arches. Wood, masonry, and plaster sculptures

The Mount Baker Theatre in Bellingham sits on a spot once occupied by two haunted houses.

and architectural features decorate every wall, doorway, and hallway throughout the theater. Faces of Spanish conquistadors, angels, nymphs, dragons, griffins, and gargoyles seem to be everywhere, and with the inevitable shadows of this huge place, they add tremendous mystique. These decorative touches and tricks of light prompted Ruth Shaw, a former theater manager to say, "From the lobby, an imaginative person looking into the orchestra pit can make out the shape of a coffin."

Reamer constructed the Mount Baker Theatre to accommodate vaudeville performers, but he wisely added a film-projection booth, anticipating the popularity of a new form of entertainment—talking pictures. To further assure the versatility of his creation, Reamer added a huge pipe organ, large orchestra pit, and several dressing rooms connected to the stage by a tunnel.

After a recent four-million-dollar renovation, the Mount Baker Theatre now has one of the best stage-performance venues in the West. Its 1,509 seats are almost always filled for concerts that range from the Pink Floyd Experience to the New Orleans Jazz Orchestra, as well as classic musical theater such as *The Three Musketeers, Oklahoma,* and *The Mikado.* Added to all this, the Mount Baker Theatre also has at least four ghosts.

Since the theater opened in 1927, ushers, film projectionists, and other staff members have reported strange experiences, especially after patrons have left the building. These experiences include gusts of cold air, balls of light, the sound of full skirts in motion, and a female voice calling out names. Much of this may be attributed to the theater's best-known ghost, Judy. This young female entity is friendly and amorous with young men. She has been known to say "good night" as male staff members leave after work and "hello" when they return the next day. She often brushes against them as they move about. Judy has been detected at many locations in the building, but she generally haunts the corridors leading to the balcony and the mezzanine. Research suggests that Judy has no direct connection with the theater. She haunts the place because it was built on a site once occupied by her house.

In the early twentieth century, the corner of Champion and Sylvan streets (now Commercial Street) was occupied by two large houses and a church. All three structures were demolished to make way for the new movie palace. Long before their destruction, one of the houses was rumored to be haunted while the other was a brothel. It is believed a young woman named Judy died in one of these houses either by a fire or murder. When ground was broken for the new construction, workmen uncovered something that was never fully disclosed. It is believed they found a shallow grave containing a female body. Her bones disturbed, the ghost became aroused and attached to the site, curious with the structure that now sits over her grave.

In September 1995, painter Garner Davies snapped a photograph in a hallway leading to the balcony. The photograph shows a transparent white mist floating a few feet off the carpeted floor and spanning the hallway. The mist is denser in the center, but it is not shaped like a person or animal. I took several digital photos at this site in May 2006, but found nothing unusual. However, an intense cold spot was detected accompanied by the swishing sound of a full skirt. Garner Davies' photograph has been widely publicized.

In 1996, after completion of major renovations, haunting activity seemed to increase. A psychic from Everett conducted a séance in the theater and identified three other ghosts—two actors and a stagehand. They tend to stay front stage left, milling about as if waiting for the curtain to rise.

The best way for ghost hunters to investigate this site is to attend a performance. This allows free access to all public spaces and an opportunity to speak to staff members. A return visit during times when the theater is empty might be arranged by speaking to the manager.

OLD TOWN CAFÉ

316 West Holly Street
Bellingham 98225
360-671-4431

This popular eatery occupies part of a building called the Overland Block. A "block" was a term used to describe a large commercial building designed to house many businesses. Construction techniques of the late nineteenth century allowed for large buildings to occupy a full city block. The owner's name was often attached, such as the Overland Block. In nearby Fairhaven, you find the Nelson Block and the Morgan Block.

Located a short distance from the historic city hall, the Overland Block was once the hub of old Bellingham's commercial sector. A mural painted on the side of a nearby building depicts the area in 1906, when the seaport was crowded with ships and the streets were filled with horse-drawn buggies.

Waitresses at the Old Town Café in Bellingham can tell you some hair-raising ghost stories.

By design, the Overland Block was home to many businesses including a rooming house, bars, a gambling hall, and a brothel or two. With this mix of seedy enterprises and the steady flow of lost souls over the decades, it is not a surprise to find a ghost or two in this building. In fact, the present-day Old Town Café is haunted by at least two ghosts.

The café is a blend of styles. To the right are small, comfortable booths with quaint touches from the 1940s and earlier. To the right is a more modern, open eating area with newer furniture and large windows that brighten the room and provide a nice view of the street. Busy waitresses dash about the place, but they often comment on the ghosts to customers. One of them mentioned to me that the place gets truly spooky with paranormal activity around Halloween.

Employees have witnessed dishes that float in the food-preparation area for as long as fifteen minutes. Others, including regular patrons, often hear piano music in the dining area to the left of the doorway. The tunes are described as old-time or honky-tonk, quite a surprise since no piano exists in the building.

People on the street, roaming from one antiques store to the next,

The ghostly image of a woman in the second-story window above the Old Town Café has been captured in photographs.

have reported seeing a woman looking at them from a second-floor window. She appears lifelike, with full cheeks and wavy, light-colored hair. She stares at mesmerized passersby and then vanishes. This apparition has been seen often by many people who frequent the neighborhood. It is believed that she lived on the premises with her husband, who owned a business in the Overland Block. It is more likely that she was a working girl in one of the upstairs brothels that flourished in the early twentieth century.

ANGEL EYES AND THE DEATH BED

Bayview Cemetery
1420 Woburn Street
Bellingham 98229
360-676-6972

The Bayview Cemetery, more than 234 acres of ground on the east side of Bellingham, has a nice view of the bay from the high ground at the abbey. Founded in 1878, the cemetery's first burials took place a year later. Many local pioneers are interred there, including Captain Henry Roeder and his wife, Elizabeth. In 1852, Roeder, with partner Russell Peabody, establish the first water-powered sawmill on nearby Whatcom Creek. Edward and Teresa Eldridge are there, too. Teresa was known as the Mother of Whatcom because she was the first white woman in this part of the state when she arrived in May 1853. Edward distinguished himself as a farmer, county official, banker, and early supporter of women's right to vote.

More than two hundred veterans of the Civil War are interred in Bayview Cemetery. Their graves surround a monument at the east side of the cemetery. At the front of the cemetery, in section C, another monument marks the resting place of twenty-three workers killed in 1895, when dynamite ignited gas at Blue Canyon mine.

Section 26 is devoted to children, anchored by a touching sculpture carved by Ruth Mueseler titled *A Child Has Died.* The sculpture is of a mother kneeing on a flat stone, surrounded by five similar stones. It was created with funds contributed by the Mother's Walk on September 10, 2000. Touching and poignant, these stones have been dubbed the death bed. Some individuals have posted notes on the Internet claiming that anyone who lies on these stones hastens their death. There is no proof or even anecdotal reports to suggest premature death follows this act of disrespect for the intent of the monument.

Sensitive visitors to the monument can hear the sweet sound of children laughing and feel a tender presence. People who kneel at the central stone and lay their hands on the shoulder of the grieving mother feel some amazing sensations. Nearby, is the grave of ten-year old Stephen Tsiorvas who was killed in 1999 when a pipeline exploded in Whatcom Park. His friend and fellow victim, Wade King, is buried in section 23.

Another paranormal location in this old cemetery is a monument called *Angel Eyes.* This tall grave marker is located in section O, next to the creek near Woburn Street. Many people have witnessed an apparition there in board daylight, believed to be the person buried beneath the statue. The monument is surrounded by small, ground-level stones engraved with the names Gertrude Bland (1890-1970) and William Bland (1869-1936). The name on another stone in this

Many stories are told of paranormal events at this sculpture, which is titled A Child Has Died *but is better known as the death bed, in Bayview Cemetery.*

group is unreadable. If you visit this site at night, bring a flashlight and move carefully. The ground is uneven, and the place is very spooky.

Information on www.theshadowlands.net mentions ghostly apparitions floating along the stone walls of the cemetery. When I visited in May 2006, I found a few walls. Near the abbey, at the Child's Court, and at a few other spots, masonry walls are evident, but they are not very old, nor are they associated with the graves of people who might be haunting the cemetery. The city of Bellingham's Web site offers detailed maps of the cemetery and a listing of graves.

IDENTIFYING THE DEAD

Good Earth Pottery
The Morgan Block
1000 Harris Avenue
Fairhaven Historic District
Bellingham 98225
360-671-3998

It was a bizarre practice that is still talked about today. In the late nineteenth century, many derelicts, bums, and deadbeats milled about the streets of Fairhaven. Several mornings each week, the local deputies would find a dead body propped up against a wall in some alley or stretched out among the weeds in a vacant lot. Many times, officers were called to a rooming house to pick up a stiff who had

This young ghost hunter examines the spot where the unidentified dead were once displayed in Fairhaven. Spirits of some of them still wait for identification.

killed himself either with alcohol, a noose, or a pistol. When no one at the scene identified the body, the corpse would be placed on a pallet at the corner of Harris Avenue and Tenth Street, where a sign requested passersby to help identify the dead.

Most of the time, no one identified the body. After a few days of display, the body was then hauled away and placed in a pauper's grave. This bizarre practice ended early in the twentieth century but has been commemorated by a concrete marker placed in the ground outside the Morgan Block, near the doorway to Good Earth Pottery. The marker reads "Unknown dead men displayed here 1901."

Spirits of bums and derelicts may hang out at this location. They may be waiting for a friend to pass by to identify them, or they may be looking for their bodies. Sensitives who visit this site after sunset feel some strange sensations. This is a good place to sit on the bench and meditate on the late-nineteenth-century time period and the lost souls who were displayed there.

Businesses established in the Morgan Block may have suffered from negative energy generated by disturbed spirits whose bodies were displayed at this site. The building was completed in 1890 and housed the Morgan House Saloon and store on the first floor. Rooms on the upper floors were originally intended to be respectable housing, but were quickly taken over by transients who patronized the bars and brothels. Instead of becoming a fine business establishment like the Waldron and Mason blocks, the Morgan Block fit in more with the seedy businesses of lower Harris Avenue. You can imagine how the display of dead bodies would keep refined citizens from visiting the place.

A BORED GHOST

The Nelson Block
Eleventh Street at Harris Avenue
Fairhaven Historic District
Bellingham 98225
Contact Three French Hens Shop, 360-756-1047

J. P. Nelson constructed this two-story building in 1900 and for thirty years operated a bank on the first floor. The second and third

The loud yawns of a bored ghost echo through the hallways of this 1900 building in Fairhaven.

floors housed professional offices, including a dentist's office during the 1940s and '50s. The few recent additions to the exterior blend well with the building's high Victorian Italianate style, which features a round-arched portal at the corner entrance. Engraved at the peak of the arch is the word "Bank," while high above it, engraved on the parapet of the corner bay, is the date of construction, 1900.

Today, a boutique—Three French Hens—and a restaurant share the ground floor. On the Eleventh Street side of the building, a formal entrance opens to a foyer and staircase that leads down to the basement or up to the second and third floors.

People working on the first floor late at night often hear the sound of someone walking around on the deserted second floor. The footsteps sound as if they are falling on crushed glass or sand. The history of the building offers no explanation for this. There was never an explosion or other disaster that shattered all the windows. Some of this auditory phenomenon might be linked to the ghost of a woman who died on the second floor. Reports state that at the age of seventeen, she died while seated in the dentist's chair. Some of the people who work in the offices on the second floor have seen the woman's partial apparition pass through closed doors. While seated on the sofa on the second-floor landing, I heard a loud sigh from the vacant space next to me. The voice was male, though, and not accompanied by a cold spot or other paranormal phenomena.

The basement used to be a meeting hall for a secret society. Human remains were found in the 1970s during renovations. The basement has an eerie atmosphere with intense cold spots and bizarre noises that resemble groans. Ghost hunters can visit the basement by speaking to employees of the restaurant.

GHOST ON THE PHONE

Rebecca's Flower Shoppe
1003 Harris Avenue
Fairhaven Historic District
Bellingham 98225
360-715-3066

This delightful flower shop occupies part of the Quinby Building. The structure blends in with the other buildings of the Fairhaven Historic District, but it is only about twenty years old. Best known for the haunted Doggie Diner, that part of the building has been replaced with an Italian restaurant. In spite of the young age of the building, Rebecca's Flower Shoppe is haunted. Built on a lot that sat vacant for several decades, no one knows why so much ghostly activity occurs in this newer building. One theory is that there are only one or two ghosts there, but they are quite active and wander throughout the three businesses in the building. It is possible, however, that there are several ghosts brought there by the artifacts, trinkets, and furniture that fill the adjoining business, Off the Wall Antiques and Interiors.

Rebecca Wiswell, owner of the flower shop, told me about a mysterious phone call she received in April 2006. While speaking on the phone to a friend, the line suddenly filled with static, like a poorly

Rebecca's Flower Shoppe in Fairhaven houses a playful ghost.

tuned radio. After a moment, Wiswell heard a woman's voice that she described as "old-time" penetrate the noise. The ghostly speaker carried on an unintelligible conversation, never pausing for a reply. After a few minutes of this bizarre intrusion, the line again filled briefly with static, then cleared as Wiswell's friend came through, clearly unaware of the interruption. Puzzled, Wiswell attributed this interruption to one of the ghosts that haunts the Quinby Building.

Fortunately, the ghost did not sound alarmed or in distress.

Other ghostly activities in Rebecca's Flower Shoppe include missing price tags. Wiswell, and others who work in the shop, sometimes find all the price tags removed from items in a particular part of the store. A day or so later, they all reappear in a little pile near the objects from which they were removed.

In the open passageway between the flower shop and the adjoining Off the Wall Antiques and Interiors, people have heard creaking door hinges. This is unnerving because there is no door at this spot.

ANTIQUES AND THEIR GHOSTS

Off the Wall Antiques and Interiors
1005 Harris Avenue
Fairhaven Historic District
Bellingham 98225
360-734-5054

Patti Lierman loves antiques, even if they come with a ghost. Her charming shop is filled with fascinating things from several past eras, including many wall-mounted mirrors and a set of French chairs. When Lierman moved into the Quinby Building in 2004, she heard about the ghost activity in the adjacent space occupied by the Doggie Diner. She was not deterred by the stories. In fact, she loves feeling the spooky connection between an antique or an old building and its past era. But the ghostly activity in Lierman's store goes far beyond what anyone would expect, even in the historic Fairhaven area.

The ghost of a Victorian woman has been seen gazing at the street through the glass of the shop's door. Last year, Mercedes, a friend of Lierman's, drove across town through bad weather and came to a stop in front of the shop, pausing to make sure the store was open before parking. Mercedes saw someone standing in the doorway and assumed Lierman was open for business. As she wheeled into a parking space, the image in the doorway became clear, revealing the details of a Victorian dress and hairstyle. Thinking this odd, Mercedes parked her car and walked to the door of the shop only to find it closed and empty of any living soul.

Patti Lierman's Off the Wall Antiques and Interiors *in Fairhaven displays choice pieces of vintage furniture, some of which comes with their own ghosts.*

At times, people in the antiques store hear the sound of someone laughing through the large opening that leads into the adjacent flower shop. Ghostly activity includes missing keys and price tags that turn up later, as well as bottles, books, and glass figures that mysteriously move from high shelves to the floor without damage. Two astonished witnesses once saw a package of crackers fly off a shelf and travel eight feet.

One particularly chilling event involved a radio-CD player. While playing a CD, the radio switched on and the speakers filled with both music and the voices of people speaking on the radio. The device is designed to make this impossible, yet this strange phenomenon continued for several minutes.

Another hair-raising event involved four French chairs that are arranged around a table near the front window. Witnesses have seen them move, slide away from the table, and make a quarter turn, as if invisible beings were seating themselves.

The Quinby Building fits nicely with the older buildings of this charming historic district. The site was a vacant lot for decades, and before that, the lot was covered with a few wooden shacks, one of which was a cigar factory. After visiting Off the Wall Antiques on two separate days, I concluded that its ghosts came in with the antiques. A similar phenomenon was documented at Spellbinding Ways Bookstore in Alameda, California, where a ghost named Louisa took up residence in the store when her favorite chair was brought to the site. In the case of Patti Lierman's ghosts, they are playful and friendly and probably look after their cherished possessions that brought them comfort and joy when they were alive.

GHOSTS OF THE SECRET SOCIETIES

Pythias Hall
1208-10 Eleventh Street
Fairhaven Historic District
Bellingham 98225
Contact Village Books, 360-671-2626, or Colophon Café, 360-647-0092

Of all the buildings in the Fairhaven Historic District, Pythias Hall looks the most haunted. When late afternoon shadows fall across the front of this tall building, strange images may be seen in the old, dirty windows of the deserted upper floors. To get closer to the ghosts of this old building, ghost hunters should visit the Colophon Café on the first floor.

The Knights of Pythias and Masonic Hall was constructed in 1891

*Members of two secret societies staged meetings and rituals in this 1891
building in Fairhaven.*

with architectural features that emulate the Richardsonian
Romanesque style. The street level has been remodeled as the
Colophon Café, but the large marquee that shades the entrance is
nearly a century old. The façade of the two upper floors features tall,
slender windows capped with faceted brick panels. These floors are
no longer used because of their deteriorated status. As stone engrav-
ings on the façade indicate, the Masons used the second floor as their
meeting hall while the Knights of Pythias occupied the top floor. In
the 1890s, the membership of these secret societies included some of
the most wealthy and influential men in the region. Many of the
architectural features of these secret meeting halls still stand. A large
portion of the upper floor shows remnants of a large ballroom. In
1893, McIntosh Hardware occupied the space that is now the
Colophon Café. In the basement, a speakeasy operated during
Prohibition. This illegal business, together with the secret societies,

probably contributed to the hauntings and ghostly happenings throughout the building.

The manager of the Colophon Café has witnessed some strange things in the ice cream shop. One night while closing, he passed down the row of booths to check the napkin holders. When he turned around, he was astonished to see that all of them had been turned ninety degrees from the position he had left them. From this area, some people have heard loud footsteps coming from the deserted second floor. At one point, the all-night bakery crew used to play loud rock music to keep spirits from leaving their musty quarters on the upper floors and visiting the busy kitchen.

A PHANTOM PASSENGER ON THE RED BUS

Jacci's Fish & Chips
1020 Harris Avenue at Eleventh Street
Fairhaven Historic District
Bellingham 98225
360-733-5021

Since its reincarnation as a fish and chips eatery, a 1948-vintage British double-decker bus has become known as a haunted place. Employees who work in the tight quarters of the main deck often hear someone walking the aisle of the upper deck when there is no chance that a curious tourist has climbed the spiral steps to the top. Creaking doors have been heard, too. No one has seen a ghost there or observed doors, windows, or other objects set in motion by invisible hands, but the sounds coming from the upper deck are creepy. One employee said the sounds are less frequent and quieter since carpeting was installed on the top deck. But the ghost is still walking around, giving everyone a chilling feeling.

It's anyone's guess as to who might be haunting this bus. Likely possibilities include a bus conductor or passenger. Over the course of many years of service, the chances that someone died on the bus are high. But little is known of the bus's history before it left merry old England to the day it showed up in Fairhaven as a popular outdoors café.

This converted British double-decker bus in Fairhaven has a few ghost passengers still waiting for their stops.

Another possible identity for this ghost is Marshal Richard Parker. According to a ground-level plaque placed at the entrance to the Red Bus garden, Parker's office used to occupy this site. According to legend, Parker left town after only one year on the job. He took with him the town's treasury and set himself up in Buenos

Aires. Speculation includes the possibility that he left part of his stolen money buried under the marshal's office where the Red Bus now sits. This may have enticed Parker's ghost to return to Fairhaven.

THE LADY IN GREEN AND GHOSTS OF THE MASON BLOCK

1200 Harris Avenue at Twelfth Street
Fairhaven Historic District
Bellingham 98225
360-733-6800

This huge commercial building was erected in 1890 at a cost of fifty thousand dollars by one of Fairhaven's first entrepreneurs, a Tacoma investor named Allen C. Mason. Its three floors and mezzanine open to an atrium that rises to the height of the building, offering expansive views of the lobby and creating an open space full of light. In its heyday, the Mason Block housed the exclusive Cascade Club, Pacific Clothing Company, Higginson-Hardy Fairhaven Pharmacy, Great Northern Express Offices, and several other professional offices. Every important Fairhaven visitor was ushered through this place and offered an opportunity to do business with the town's leading businessmen. After hours, the town's exclusive men's club, the Cascade Club, hosted such notables as President William Howard Taft and Mark Twain. At times, apartments were established on the upper floors, allowing businessmen to work close to their families.

For many years, the Mason Block was the leading place for business in Fairhaven. But for all the comings and goings, only one person is known to have died in the building. Flora Blakely was the wife of town marshal Joseph Blakely. They lived in an apartment on the fourth floor of the Mason Block with their daughter. In 1892, Flora died in her bedroom while giving birth to their second child. Her funeral, staged in the lobby of the Mason Block, attracted every member of Fairhaven's upper crust. After many tearful good-byes, her body was transported to

Several ghosts haunt the Mason Block in Fairhaven, including the famous Lady in Green, Flora Blakely, who died there in 1892.

Brownsville, Oregon, for burial. But this popular lady loved her Fairhaven home so much that she has remained there for more than a century after her death.

As early at 1893, residents and workers in the building began to notice strange happenings immediately attributed to the ghost of Flora Blakely. To this day, the building is known as a haunted place, but this has not detracted from the survival of the Mason Block as a successful commercial center.

For more than a century, people have noticed oddly shaped shadows move along the second- and third-floor corridors, as well as unexplained reflections of light on the staircases. Some people have seen bottles and glasses taking flight or inexplicably falling from a table. Chairs are sometimes rearranged, intense cold spots appear, and eerie sensations are felt, as though you are being watched by an invisible being. The sounds of laughter and rattling of glass windows have unnerved people for many decades. More recently, ghosts have tampered with computers and printers that had been turned off in the evening, only to be found turned on in the morning with all of their paper passed through the machines and scattered on the floor.

Members of the Washington State Ghost Hunting Society have recorded some amazing EVP, and psychics have channeled some fascinating characters who have taken up residence in Sycamore Square long after their death. Much of the ghostly activity in this building has been attributed to Flora Blakely. While working late one night, a building manager spotted her apparition. The witness first stepped into a cold spot and then experienced that scary feeling that she was not alone in the room. Turning to face what she thought was an intruder, the shaking witness saw a young woman in a green velvet Victorian-style dress. She appeared fully formed, but not quite lifelike. After a few moments of amazement, the witness watched as the ghost disappeared. Later, some photographs revealed orbs and digital images believed to be a manifestation of Flora Blakely's spirit.

On the top floor, where Flora once lived, some ghost hunters have used a low-tech effort to detect ghostly activity by placing chairs with their backs to the window. In the morning, the chairs are rearranged facing the windows that offer a beautiful view of Bellingham Bay. It is believed Flora turned the chairs.

Psychics have encountered other ghosts in this building. A young woman named Abigail haunts the Black Cat, a French cabaret on the third floor. This ghost loves to dance and wear large hats. On the fourth floor, the ghost of a former member of the men-only Cascade Club does not like women entering this space. Ella

Higginson, former resident of the Mason Block and wife of the Fairhaven Pharmacy proprietor, may be haunting the building, too. Her photograph hangs with many other historic photos on the walls of the upper-floor corridors.

In the lobby, I encountered the pale, partial apparition of an elderly female who is profoundly sad. She was a relative of Flora Blakely and attended the funeral there in 1892. Her spirit walks around the fountain, twisting a handkerchief in her hands, overcome with grief.

Ghost hunters interested in the Mason Block may access a list of building residents from the 1890s, plus the early history of the place and photographs of some fascinating characters at www.sycamore square.com. Statements by people who have encountered ghosts at the Mason Block are also available.

AFTERGLOW MAUSOLEUM

Afterglow Drive at Cessna Avenue
Friday Harbor 98250-7113
Contact San Juan County Cemetery District, 360-378-2065

This burial monument is one of the most fascinating and bizarre in the Pacific Northwest. It was conceived by John Stafford McMillin (1855-1936), owner of the Hotel de Haro, Roche Harbor Lime and Cement Co., and most of the town of Roche Harbor. Built primarily as a depository for his remains and those of his wife and four children, the mausoleum stands as a testimony to his beliefs, dreams, and aspirations.

The architecture of the Afterglow Mausoleum consists of symbolism based on Masonic and Knights Templar philosophy. A stone table sits in the center, the eternal meeting place of the family at the end of each day. The six chairs at the table not only provide seating for each member of the family, but also hold the ashes of the deceased. Seven columns surround the table, but the seventh, standing on the west side of the monument, was left unfinished as though broken, representing man's work interrupted and unfinished by death. The number of steps leading to the monument represents several philosophies, including the five orders of architecture, the three stages of human life—youth, adulthood, and old age—and the seven liberal arts and sciences. The upper border of fleurs-de-lis, a Knights Templar symbol, is carved seven times into the ring that connects the seven columns. Some of the symbolism is a mystery to visitors, but recognized by high-ranking Masons. McMillin and his son, Fred, were thirty-second-degree Masons.

The fascinating monument appears perfect, but it is incomplete. McMillin's original design included a bronze dome topped with a Maltese cross. For unknown reasons, his descendents did not commission the installation of this final piece.

McMillin's passion for this project was so strong that many believe his spirit resides at this place together with the spirits of his wife, Louella Hiett McMillin (1857-1943), and their children, infant John (1878), Dorothy (1894-1980), Paul (1886-1961), and Fred (1880-1922). Many people who have visited the Afterglow Mausoleum during a full moon claim to have seen members of the McMillin family seated in their chairs, as if they were gathered for dinner. By daylight, the place is no less mysterious or spooky. Sensitive people feel the presence of unseen entities near the table. Those who dare to sit in the chairs of the deceased feel uneasy, and then they experience a dreaded sense of having violated something. Those who push their luck and sit on the table may feel invisible hands push them off.

The spirit energy at this tomb is so strange and powerful that people who have entered the monument and sat in the chairs while it was raining have noticed that no rain falls on them. It is as if John McMillin's bronze canopy is in place, sheltering the area from the weather.

During a visit to San Juan Island, ghost hunters should visit the University of Washington Marine Biological Laboratories at Friday Harbor. Some of the buildings, once part of a naval station, are believed to be haunted. Doors and windows open by unseen hands. Shadows have been seen that resemble those of Native Americans. Also visit the Hotel de Haro at Roche Harbor. John McMillin once owned this building. The apparition of a middle-age woman wearing a long dress may be seen on the second floor. Many believe she was a housekeeper or maid.

GHOST OF THE WILD WOMAN ALICE RHEEM

Rosario Resort & Spa
1400 Rosario Road
Eastsound 98245
800-562-8820
www.rosarioresort.com/

The man who built the mansion now known as Rosario Resort & Spa had a curious history that suggests he might be haunting the place. By the time Robert Moran, born in New York City in 1857, was eighteen years old, he knew his future was to be found somewhere out West. In 1875 he arrived at the muddy little sawmill town on the shores of Puget Sound called Seattle. Within days he landed a job on Yesler's dock loading lumber on schooners bound for San Francisco.

By 1887, Moran had worked his way into what amounted to an executive position and won a seat on the city council. With the social and political advantages of his role in government he became a rich man. All of this, including his marriage to Melissa Paul of Canada, came to a crashing halt in 1906 when Moran's doctor diagnosed him with a terminal disease. At age forty-nine, given only one year to live, he abandoned his political career and built his dream house on Orcas Island. As soon as Moran settled into a sublime lifestyle, he noticed improved health. In fact, he felt so good that in 1913, six years after his anticipated death, he added a twenty-six-rank Aeolian pipe organ to his mansion. The 1,972 pipes filled the huge mansion with an astonishing sound.

Robert Moran finally died in 1926, a rich and happy man. Many would think that this history would lead to a haunting. In fact several ghost hunters have searched the place for Moran's ghost, although without much success. The spirit that many have found there is a female with her own fascinating history.

In 1926, Donald and Alice Rheem were a prominent San Francisco couple. He was a business magnate known for turning a quick buck amid troubled financial waters. It is said that Alice was a drunk. Even in the days of Prohibition, she found every speakeasy in town, pouring thousands of dollars into the bootleg industry. In a town like San Francisco, Donald found it was impossible to keep the lid on Alice's drinking problem as well as her escapades with other men. He packed up her things, dragged her aboard a train, and headed north to a secluded place he had purchased on Orcas Island. When Alice sobered up, she found herself in Robert Moran's Orcas Island mansion.

It turns out that the big house on East Sound didn't stop Alice from drinking and carrying on with wild parties. Every time Donald left on a business trip, the phonograph blared, lights blazed, and the gin flowed like water. Eventually this lifestyle caught up with Alice, and she died of the effects of her alcoholism in 1937.

Alice's ghost may be too drunk to realize that she is dead. After the mansion became an inn, people noticed the sounds of bedsprings and soft moans as they lay in bed at night. This passionate spirit seems to replay adventures between the sheets with her many illicit lovers. Others have seen a woman, barely covered by a red nightgown, walk across their room, then pass through a wall. This ghost also appears in the hallways of the second floor and on the small deck that overlooks the bay.

Psychic investigation of the Rosario Resort reveals an intense sadness and careless attitude about life that fits with descriptions of Alice Rheem. Her ghost roams the place with a strong energy, looking for yet another party in spite of the alcoholism that took her life.

Other places in communities north of Seattle for ghost hunting:

THE HISTORIC SHIP *EQUATOR*

Tenth Street Boat Launch Facility
Everett 98201

Little remains of this once glorious seventy-six-ton ship built in 1888, except the hull that looks like it might fall apart at any time. The shed that protects the eighty-one-foot ship from the weather also prevents access, but serious ghost hunters can contact the local historical society for a close look at this haunted ship. The ghosts of writer Robert Louis Stevenson and Hawaiian King Kalakaua have been detected abroad this maritime relic by psychics who conducted a séance. In 1888, Stevenson chartered the ship for a six-month cruise of the South Pacific. Some believe the hull is protected by the ghosts of sailors who once served near the equator.

SHUKSAN REHAB

1530 James Street
Bellingham 98225
360-733-9161

This nursing home is reported to be haunted. Two registered nurses saw a ghost walk through a door while several others—staff, patients, and visitors—have witnessed objects move, heard bizarre noises, and felt the presence of unseen beings.

WARDNER'S CASTLE/HILLTOP HOUSE

1103 Fifteenth Street at Knox Avenue
Fairhaven Historic District
Bellingham 98225

This twenty-three-room mansion used to be the Castle's Bed and Breakfast, providing ghosts hunters with a thrilling night's stay in an authentic haunted house. It is now a private residence, but serious ghost hunters may contact the residents for permission to look around. The place was built in 1890 by Jim Wardner, who became known as a crazy cat man. Wardner raised cats and sold their pelts disguised as furs from prized animals. Later, residents of the house reported cat ghosts and the odor of Wardner's pipe tobacco. In the 1920s, a woman died in the upstairs bedroom while giving birth. Many have heard her screams and detected her grieving husband. He appears sitting on the edge of the beds, holding his head in his hands.

MANNINO'S BELLA CUCINA

Formerly the Doggie Diner
1007 Harris Avenue
Fairhaven Historic District
Bellingham 98225
360-671-7955

The Doggie Diner used to occupy part of the Quinby Building. In its place is a popular Italian restaurant. Doggie Diner employees were sometimes too frightened to work. They reported the sound of drawers being pulled open in the upstairs office, objects falling from shelves, and a chair rolling across the floor. Some have heard babies crying in the upstairs room, now a dining room. People who eat at the restaurant can wander around and investigate the upstairs dining room, which used to be Benton's Bath Parlor and Tonsorial Palace.

FAIRHAVEN PUB

Finnegan's Alley
1114 Harris Avenue
Fairhaven Historic District
Bellingham 98225
360-671-6745

The exterior of this building displays architectural features of the early 1900s that indicate the place was once a garage. But the pub is a modern night spot, complete with fancy lighting and a black tiled floor. A blurred vision has appeared in a glass door and turned the television on and off. An employee also reported getting an affectionate hug from an unseen spirit.

THE FORMER BELLINGHAM BAY HOTEL

907-09 Harris Avenue
Fairhaven Historic District
Bellingham 98225

Two businesses occupy this building now, but the Bellingham Bay Hotel used to be a popular stop for travelers because it was close to the former red-light district and the waterfront. In the early twentieth century, several prostitutes lived in the building and attracted a rowdy crowd. Some of these rambunctious souls are still on the premises.

DOS PADRES RESTAURANT

1111 Harris Avenue
Fairhaven Historic District
Bellingham 98225
360-733-9900
www.dospadres.com

Situated across the street from the Fairhaven Pub, this Mexican restaurant and adjoining cantina occupy a building that was constructed in 1929 and used as a brothel. The place is so haunted that photographs of ghosts are on display in the bar. A shooting took place there in the early 1930s that may have involved a woman and a man in a tall hat. These ghostly figures have been seen there often. Many patrons hear odd noises, notice shadows at the edge of their vision, lose objects only to find them reappear a short time later, and see doors open and close by unseen hands.

Sighting Report Form

Photocopy and enlarge the form on the next page to a standard 8.5 x 11 inch format. This form should be completed right after a sighting. If the ghost hunt is performed by a group, a designated leader should assume the role of reporter. The reporter is responsible for completing this form.

The reporter and each witness should make a statement, either audio or written, describing in full their experience at the site. Date, sign, and label these statements with a reference number identical to the report number on the sighting report form. Attach the statements to the report form.

SIGHTING REPORT

SITE NAME _____ REPORT # _____
LOCATION _____ DATE: _____
_____ TIME: _____
REPORTER _____ SITE # _____
WITNESSES _____
_____

DESCRIPTION OF APPARITION
_____
_____

temperature change   [] YES   [] NO
auditory phenomena   [] YES   [] NO
telekinesis   [] YES   [] NO
visual phenomena   [] YES   [] NO
other phenomena   [] YES   [] NO
Description: _____

Use the reverse side for diagrams, maps, and drawings.

SPECIFIC LOCATION WITHIN SITE: _____

PREVIOUS SIGHTINGS AT THIS SITE?
                        [] YES   [] NO
Reference:
_____

Summary:
_____
_____

RECORDS:
audio   [] YES   [] NO   Ref. No. _____
video   [] YES   [] NO   Ref. No. _____
photo   [] YES   [] NO   Ref. No. _____
Summary of Records:
_____

Disposition of Records:
_____

WITNESS STATEMENTS (Summary): _____
_____

audio   [] YES   [] NO
written   [] YES   [] NO
Disposition of statements: _____
_____

Suggested Reading

BOOKS

Allison, Ross and Joe Teeples. *Ghostology 101: Becoming a Ghost Hunter.* Authorhouse, 2005.

Auerbach, Loyd. *ESP, Hauntings, and Poltergeists.* New York: Warner Books, 1986.

——. *Ghost Hunting: How to Investigate the Paranormal.* Oakland, CA: Ronin Publishing, 2004.

Bardens, Dennis. *Ghosts and Hauntings.* Lincoln, NE: IUniverse, 2000.

Beckett, John. *World's Weirdest True Ghost Stories.* New York: Sterling Publishing, 1992.

Belanger, Jeff. *The World's Most Haunted Places: From the Secret Files of Ghostvillage.com.* New Page Books, 2004.

Browne, Sylvia. *Adventures of a Psychic.* New York: Penguin Books, 1990.

Cohen, Daniel. *The Encyclopedia of Ghosts.* New York: Dodd, Mead Publishers, 1984.

Cornell, Tony. *Investigating the Paranormal.* New York: Helix Press, 2002.

Davis, Jefferson. *Haunted Tour Guide of the Pacific Northwest.* Norseman Ventures, 2003.

Dwyer, Jeff. *Ghost Hunter's Guide to Los Angeles.* Gretna, LA: Pelican Publishing Co., 2007.

——. *Ghost Hunter's Guide to New Orleans.* Gretna, LA: Pelican Publishing Co., 2007.

——. *Ghost Hunter's Guide to the San Francisco Bay Area.* Gretna, LA: Pelican Publishing Co., 2005.

Hauck, Dennis William. *Haunted Places: The National Directory.* New York: Penguin Group, 2002.

Holzer, Hans. *Ghosts I've Met.* New York: Barnes and Noble, 2005.

—. *Ghosts: True Encounters with the World Beyond.* New York: Black Dog and Leventhal Publishers, 2004.

—. *Hans Holzer's Travel Guide to Haunted Houses.* New York: Black Dog and Leventhal Publishers, 1999.

—. *Real Hauntings.* New York: Barnes and Noble, 1995.

—. *True Ghost Stories.* Barnes and Noble Books, 2001.

MacKenzie, Andrew. *Hauntings and Apparitions.* London: Granada Publishing, 1982.

Martinez, Raymond J. *Marie Laveau, Voodoo Queen.* Gretna, LA: Pelican Publishing Co., 2001.

Mead, Robin. *Haunted Hotels: A Guide to American and Canadian Inns and Their Ghosts.* Nashville: Rutledge Hill Press, 1995.

Ramsland, Katherine. *Ghost: Investigating the Other Side.* New York: St. Martin's Press, 2001.

Rule, Leslie. *Coast to Coast Ghosts: True Stories of Hauntings Across America.* Kansas City, MO: Andrews McMeel Publishing, 2001.

Smith, Barbara. *Ghost Stories of Washington.* Renton, WA: Lone Pine Publishing, 2000.

Southall, Robert. *How to be a Ghost Hunter.* St. Paul, Llewellyn Publications, 2003.

Speidel, William C. *Doc Maynard: The Man Who Invented Seattle.* Nettle Creek Publishing Co., 1978.

—. *Sons of the Profits.* Nettle Creek Publishing Co., 2003.

Steiger, Brad. *Real Ghosts, Restless Spirits, and Haunted Places.* Detroit: Visible Ink Press, 2003.

Taylor, Troy. *Ghost Hunter's Guidebook.* Alton, IL: Whitechapel Productions Press, 1999.

Warren, Joshua P. *How to Hunt for Ghosts: A Practical Guide.* New York: Fireside Press, 2003.

Winer, Richard. *Ghost Ships: True Stories of Nautical Nightmares, Hauntings, and Disasters.* New York: Berkeley Publishing Group, 2000.

ARTICLES

Associated Press. "Ghost buster: Ohio woman inspires CBS' supernatural series." *Boston Herald,* July 4, 2005.

Baldwin, Matthew. "Strangers in the night." *Seattle Morning News,* October 30, 2003.

Barrett, Greg. "Can the living talk to the dead? Psychics say they connect with the other world, but skeptics respond: 'Prove it.'" *USA Today,* June 20, 2001.

Cadden, Mary. "Get spooked on a walking tour." *USA Today,* October 17, 2003.

Chansanchai, Athima. "TV crew wants scary? Seattle has scary." *Seattle Post-Intelligencer,* September 8, 2005.

Fox, Carol. "Ghostbuster to tell secrets of the hunt." *Los Angeles Times,* October 28, 1989.

Gisi, Michelle. "Ghost hunters group asked to investigate." *Kent Reporter,* January 15, 2003.

Godden, Jean. "Seattle's spirits get visit." *Seattle Times,* June 13, 2003.

Hill, Angela. "Paranormal experts say it's not all funny." *Oakland (CA) Tribune,* October 18, 2002.

Holt, Gordy. "Wawaona becomes a ghost ship." *Seattle Post-Intelligencer,* May 4, 2005.

Jones, Monika. "Knowing the unknown." *University of Washington Daily,* August 20, 2003.

Keller, Jessica. "Plateau cemeteries draw ghost hunters." *Courier Herald,* October 20, 2003.

Kim, Gina. "Touring the ghostly sites of Seattle's Pike Place Market." *Seattle Times,* October 20, 2003.

"Loyd Auerback shares tales from the dark side." *San Francisco Chronicle,* October 30, 1998.

Loar, Russell. "She's there when things go bump in the night." *Los Angeles Times,* May 26, 1997.

Martin, Jonathan. "Historic castle (plus ghosts) destined for highest bidder." *Seattle Times,* May 10, 2004.

Massingill, T. "Business of ghost busting." *Contra Costa Times,* October 8, 2000.

Moran, Gwen. "Real-life ghost busters." *USA Weekend,* October 31, 2004.

Murakami, Kery. "Ghost tour keeps alive the spirit of oral tradition. Walking and talking at Pike Place Market." *Seattle Post-Intelligencer,* November 30, 2005.

Nowacki, Kim. "Here's how real ghost-hunters work." *Yakima Herald-Republic,* October 20, 2003.

Parvaz, D. "Mysteries lurk between the walls of Capitol Hill museum." *Seattle Post-Intelligencer,* January 31, 2005.

Robinson, Sean. "Psychics of soul searching." *Seattle News Tribune,* October 20, 2003.

"Spirits, specters and strange sightings abound at America's most haunted hotels." *Los Angeles Times,* October 15, 2003.

Sullivan, Jennifer. "Spirits soar at conclave on UFOs, paranormal." *Seattle Times,* May 26, 2003.

Sullivan, Patrick. "Ghost hunters conference here in November." *Port Townsend Leader,* August 3, 2005.

Swift, Mary. "Team on spooky mission to Kent museum." *Seattle South County Journal,* December 12, 2002.

Warne, Nathan. "AGHOST at the U-District." *University of Washington Daily,* October 30, 2003.

APPENDIX C

Films, DVDs, and Videos

Fictional films may provide information that will assist you in preparing yourself for a ghost hunt. This assistance ranges from putting you in the proper mood for ghost hunting to useful techniques for exploring haunted places and information about the nature of ghostly activity.

The Amityville Horror (1979). Directed by Stuart Rosenberg. Starring James Brolin and Margot Kidder.

Carrie (1976). Directed by Brian De Palma. Starring Sissy Spacek and Piper Laurie.

Cemetery Man (1994). Directed by Michele Soavi. Starring Rupert Everett and Francois Hadji-Lazaro.

Changeling (1980). Directed by Peter Medak. Starring George C. Scott and Trish VanDevere.

City of Angels (1998). Directed by Brad Silberling. Starring Nicolas Cage and Meg Ryan.

Dragonfly (2002). Directed by Tom Shadyac. Starring Kevin Costner and Kathy Bates.

The Entity (1983). Directed by Sidney J. Furie. Starring Barbara Hershey and Ron Silver.

Frighteners (1996). Directed by Peter Jackson. Starring Michael J. Fox and Trini Alvarado.

Ghost (1990). Directed by Jerry Zucker. Starring Patrick Swayze and Demi Moore.

Ghost of Flight 409 (1987). Made for TV. Directed by Steven Hilliard Stern. Starring Ernest Borgnine and Kim Basinger.

Ghost Ship (2002). Directed by Steve Beck. Starring Julianna Margulies and Ron Eldard.

Ghosts of California (2003). Documentary.

Ghosts of England and Belgrave Hall (2001). Documentary.

Ghost Stories, Volumes 1 and 2 (1997). Documentaries hosted by Patrick McNee.

Ghost Story (1981). Directed by John Irvin. Starring Fred Astaire and Melvyn Douglas.

Haunted (1995). Directed by Lewis Gilbert. Starring Aidan Quinn and Kate Beckinsale.

Haunted History. History Channel Home Video. Documentary.

Haunted History of Halloween. History Channel Home Video. Documentary.

Haunted Houses. A & E Home Video. Documentary.

Haunted Places (2001). Documentary by Christopher Lewis.

The Haunting (1999). Directed by Jan de Bont. Starring Liam Neeson and Catherine Zeta-Jones.

Haunting Across America (2001). Documentary hosted by Michael Dorn.

The Haunting of Hell House (1999). Starring Michael York and Claudia Christian.

The Haunting of Julia (1976). Directed by Richard Loncraine. Starring Mia Farrow and Keir Dullea.

The Haunting of Sarah Hardy (1989). Directed by Jerry London. Starring Sela Ward, Michael Woods, and Morgan Fairchild.

The Haunting of Seacliff Inn (1995). Directed by Walter Klenhard. Starring Ally Sheedy and William R. Moses.

Hollywood Ghosts and Gravesites (2003). Documentary.

Lady in White (1988). Directed by Frank LaLoggia. Starring Lukas Haas and Len Cariou.

The Legend of Hell House (1998). Directed by John Hough. Starring Pamela Franklin, Roddy MacDowell, and Clive Revill.

Living With the Dead (2000). Directed by Stephen Gyllenhaal. Starring Ted Danson and Mary Steenburgen.

The Others (2001). Directed by Alejandro Amenábar. Starring Nicole Kidman and Christopher Eccleston.

Poltergeist (1982). Directed by Tobe Hooper. Starring JoBeth Williams and Craig T. Nelson.

Poltergeist II: The Other Side (1986). Directed by Brian Gibson. Starring JoBeth Williams and Craig T. Nelson.

Restless Spirits (1999). Directed by David Wellington. Starring Lothaire Bluteau, Michel Monty, and Marsha Mason.

Sightings: Heartland Ghost (2002). Directed by Brian Trenchard-Smith. Starring Randy Birch and Beau Bridges.

The Sixth Sense (1999). Directed by M. Night Shyamalan. Starring Bruce Willis and Haley Joel Osment.

The Skeleton Key (2005). Directed by Iain Softley. Starring Kate Hudson and Gina Rowlands.

Thirteen Ghosts (2001). Directed by Steve Beck. Starring Tony Shalhoub.

White Noise (2005). Directed by Geoffrey Sax. Starring Michael Keaton.

The following two movies are not about ghosts, but they are worth watching before visiting Seattle. They provide a sneak preview of some of the scenery and a bit of local culture.

Double Jeopardy (1999). Directed by Bruce Beresford. Starring Tommy Lee Jones and Ashley Judd.

Sleepless in Seattle (1993). Directed by Nora Ephron. Starring Tom Hanks and Meg Ryan.

APPENDIX D

Special Tours and Events

Fairhaven Historic District Walking Tour. Tour the restored historic district of one of Washington's most prosperous nineteenth-century communities. Several buildings in this community have been investigated as haunted sites. Call 360-738-1574.

Ghost Tours of the Pike Place Market. Tour this Seattle landmark with guide Mercedes Yaeger, who literally grew up in the market. She tells stories about the characters and events that made the market place so unique. Keeping the tradition of oral history alive, Yaeger talks about the ghosts and paranormal happenings and reveals some secrets about Seattle's first mortuary and largest brothel. Meeting place varies. Reservations are recommended as groups are limited to twenty people Call 206-322-1218. Web site: www.marketghost.com.

Haunted Fairhaven Self-Guided Tour. At nearly every business on Harris Avenue, you can pick up a pamphlet with information to more than a dozen haunted sites in this historic town. Addresses and historical background are given, which make the tour easy and interesting. Web site: www.fairhaven.com.

Navy Warship Tours. Tour the USS *Turner Joy* (DD-951), a Vietnam-era destroyer. Spaces from the boiler room to the bridge are open to visitors, including ghost hunters. Located at 124 Washington Avenue in Bremerton, the warship display can be reached easily by a one-hour ferryboat cruise from Seattle. The ferryboat dock in Bremerton is adjacent to the Bremerton Memorial

Ship Museum and the destroyer's dock. $8. Call 360-792-2457.

Pacific Northwest Ghost Hunters Conference. This annual event is staged by the Advanced Ghost Hunters of Seattle-Tacoma (AGHOST) in the fall. The program of speakers and demonstrations attracts ghost hunters from all over the West Coast. Special tours of haunted sites are included in this three-day event. This rare gathering of local experts offers new ghost hunters a chance to learn skills and techniques and establish connections with people in the paranormal field. Call 253-203-4383. E-mail: aghost@aghost.us.

Port Townsend Living History Walking Tour. Conducted by the Jefferson County Historical Society, this one-hour stroll takes you through Port Townsend's historic district. The tour provides a good orientation for ghost hunters. Call 360-385-1003. E-mail: marsha@jchsmuseum.org.

Private Eye Haunted Happenings: Seattle Ghost Tour. Board a minivan with a knowledgeable tour guide for a two-and-a-half- to three-hour tour of central Seattle's haunted sites, including the Wah Mee Massacre of 1983, Pike Place Market, Elegant Hotel, an old burial ground, the Georgetown poor farm, and more. Pick up can be arranged at a hotel or restaurant. $20. Call 206-365-3739. Web site: www.privateeyetours.com/haunted.htm.

Private Eye Mystery and Murder Tour. This tour takes you to several of Seattle's most fascinating crime scenes, where villains were caught, victims discovered, and clues were unraveled. Highlights include examination of evidence, including the serving fork used by the "Great Raoul" to cook and eat his wife and child. Tour spans one and a half to two and a half hours. You may select a tour of Queen Anne Hill (locale for murderer Ted Bundy) or Capitol Hill. $20-25. Call 206-365-3739. Web site: www.privateeyetours.com.

Seattle Underground Tour. Dirt! Corruption! Scandal! Discover all of this in Seattle's mysterious underground city. This leisurely guided walking tour takes you to the sidewalks, storefronts, and brothels of old Seattle. Knowledgeable guides keep you entertained with stories of the city's notorious past, political foibles and corruption, and most colorful characters. The tour ends with a visit to Rogues Gallery, where you can see photographs of people whose ghost may still haunt the underground city. Tour meets at Doc Maynard's Lounge on Pioneer Square, 608 First Avenue, Seattle. $11. Call 206-682-4646.

See Seattle Walking Tours. This six-hour tour offers a great opportunity to get oriented to the city. The easy-paced tour traces the path of Chief Seattle and the Great Fire and several other locations of historic events. Meet at the outdoor seating area of Westbrook Plaza, at Fourth Avenue and Pine Street near the Starbucks, at 10:00 a.m. Tour ends at 4:00 p.m. Call 425-226-7641. Web site: www.seeseattle.com. Fee: $20.00 plus fees for streetcar ($1.25), Smith Tower observation deck ($6.00), and lunch ($7-9.00)

Thornewood Castle Candle Light Mystery Tour. Three to four special tours are staged at this huge castle each year. Deanna Robinson, co-owner and hostess, escorts visitors through long corridors and special rooms in search of ghosts. She shares stories about the castle's builder and first family and the Native Americans who built the mansion. Tours are four hours and limited to overnight guests. Contact the castle for specific dates and times. $100 plus room charge for one night. Call 253-584-4393. Web site: www.thornewoodcastle.com.

Tillicum Indian Village on Blake Island. Cruise from Seattle's Pier 55 to Blake Island for a salmon bake and demonstrations of local Indian cultural, including a stage production called *Dance on the Wind.* This four-hour excursion also affords an opportunity to visit the remains of the Blake mansion, which burned in 1960. The island is also available for hiking and camping. $69. Call 206-933-8600 or 800-426-1205. Web site: www.blakeislandadventures.com.

Organizations

You may contact these organizations to report ghost phenomena, obtain advice, or arrange for an investigation of a haunting. Many of these organizations conduct conferences, offer training, or list educational opportunities for those seeking to become paranormal investigators.

Advanced Ghost Hunters of Seattle-Tacoma (AGHOST)
253-203-4383
E-mail: aghost@aghost.us
www.aghost.us/

American Society for Psychical Research
5 West 73rd Street
New York, NY 10023
212-799-5050

Berkeley Psychic Institute
2436 Hastings Street
Berkeley, CA 94704
510-548-8020

British Society for Psychical Research
Eleanor O'Keffe, secretary
49 Marloes Road
London W86LA
England
44-71-937-8984

Committee for Scientific Investigations of Claims of the Paranormal
1203 Kensington Avenue
Buffalo, NY 14215

Division of Parapsychology
Box 152, Medical Center
Charlottesville, VA 22908

Ghost Hunters of the South (GHOTS)
www.ghots.net

Institute for Parapsychology
Box 6847
College Station
Durham, NC 27708

International Ghost Hunters Society
www.ghostweb.com

International Society for Paranormal Research
4712 Admiralty Way
Marina del Rey, CA 90292

Louisiana Paranormal Research Society
725 Misty Lane
Lake Charles, LA 70611

Office of Paranormal Investigations
John F. Kennedy University
12 Altarinda Road
Orinda, CA 94563
415-249-9275

Orange County Paranormal Research Group
E-mail: OCPR@OCPRgroup.com
www.ocprgroup.com

San Diego Paranormal Research Project
E-mail: Info@SDparanormal.com
www.SDparanormal.com

Southern California Society for Psychical Research
269 South Arden Boulevard
Los Angeles, CA 90004

Stanford University
Department of Psychology
Jordan Hall, Building 420
Stanford, CA 94305

Washington State Ghost Society
www.washingtonstateghostsociety.com

APPENDIX F

Internet Resources

www.aghost.us/. Advanced Ghost Hunters of Seattle-Tacoma is a well-organized, highly active group of researchers, investigators, and consultants. AGHOST has been featured on several television programs. The group stages the annual Pacific Northwest Ghost Hunter's Conference in the fall.

www.ghosthunter.com. Web site of ghost hunter and lecturer Patti Starr.

www.ghostresearch.org. The Ghost Research Society was established in 1971 as a clearing house for reports of paranormal activity. Members research homes and businesses and analyze photographs and audio and video recordings to determine authenticity. Headed by well-known ghost researcher Dale Kaczmarek.

www.ghost-stalker.com. Richard Senate is a well-known author, lecturer, and ghost investigator who focuses mainly on Southern California locations.

www.ghoststore.net. This Web site is a catalog listing a vast array of ghost hunting equipment available for purchase.

www.ghosttowns.com. Informative Web site that gives detailed information about ghost towns in the U. S. and Canada.

www.ghostweb.com. The International Ghost Hunters Society, headed by Drs. Sharon Gill and Dave Oester, researches spirits to produce evidence of life after death. The society offers a home-study certification for paranormal investigators. Membership exceeds 15,000 people.

www.ghots.net. Web site of Ghost Hunters of the South; an association of researchers and investigators.

www.hauntings.com. Web site of the International Society for Paranormal Research.

www.historichotels.org. Historic hotels of America are detailed here.

www.history.com. Official Web site of the History Channel

www.hollowhill.com. A ghost-information Web site that displays reports, photographs, eye-witness reports, location information, and ghost-hunting techniques.

www.ispr.net/home.html. The International Society for Paranormal Research, headed by Dr. Larry Montz, conducts ghost expeditions, provides the media with expert opinions on paranormal issues, and lists classes and products of interest to ghost hunters.

www.jeffdwyer.com. Web site of paranormal investigator, ghost hunter, and writer Jeff Dwyer.

www.marylandghosts.com. The Maryland Ghost and Spirit Association, founded by Beverly Litsinger, investigates Civil War sites in Maryland, Virginia, Pennsylvania, and other haunted locations.

www.mindreader.com. The Office of Paranormal Investigations is directed by internationally known author and researcher Loyd Auerbach. The office investigates a variety of paranormal activity for a fee. Information about current and former investigations is available to serious researchers and the media.

www.nationalghosthunters.com/investigations.html. Official Web site of the National Ghost Hunters Society. This organization of psychics and mediums helps people solve problems with ghosts.

www.nps.gov. Web site of the National Park Service, which lists several hundred historic sites.

www.paranormality.com/ghost_hunting_equipment.shtml. The Web site displays high-tech equipment useful in paranormal investigations.

www.prarieghosts.com. Official Web site of the American Ghost Society, founded by author and ghost researcher Troy Taylor. This site provides information about ghost research, paranormal investigations, and books written by Troy Taylor.

www.psiapplications.com. PSI is a northern California organization dedicated to the investigation and documentation of anomalous events, including the paranormal.

www.scghs.com. Web site of the Southern California Ghost Hunters Society. This organization performs investigations of haunted locations and provides consultations.

www.the-atlantic-paranormal-society.com. Official Web site of the Atlantic Paranormal Society (TAPS). This group of ghost investigators gained fame through the Sci Fi channel program *Ghost Hunters.*

www.theshadowlands.net/ghost. Directory of reports of unsubstantiated hauntings and other paranormal events organized by state. This is a good Web site for finding places that might be hot spots for ghostly activity.

www.undergroundtour.com. Web site of the Seattle underground tour, Rogues Gallery museum and store, and Doc's Lounge. This site gives information and schedules for the underground tour and contact information for private tours.

www.washingtonstateghostsociety.com. The Washington State Ghost Society is a nonprofit organization that assists individuals who have experienced paranormal phenomena.

www.yahoo.com. Online map service that includes driving instructions. Click on "Maps,", enter your starting address, then enter the address of the haunted place you wish to visit. Yahoo will generate a free map and driving instructions, including estimated driving time and total miles.

Historical Societies and Museums

Historical societies and museums are good places to discover information about old houses and other buildings or places that figure prominently in local history. They often contain records in the form of old newspapers, diaries, and photographs about tragic events such as fires, hangings, train wrecks, and earthquakes that led to the loss of life. Old photographs and maps that are not on display for public viewing may be available to serious researchers.

Anacortes Museum
1305 Eighth Street
Anacortes, WA 98221
360-293-1915

Bainbridge Island Historical Museum
P.O. Box 11653
7650 Northeast High School Road
Bainbridge Island, WA 98110
260-842-2773

Bremerton Naval Museum
130 Washington Avenue
Bremerton, WA 98337
360-479-7447

Des Moines Historical Society
730 South 225th Street

Des Moines, WA 99198
206-824-5226

Edmonds Museum
118 Fifth Avenue
Edmonds, WA 98020
425-774-0900

Everett Museum
2915 Hewitt Avenue
Everett, WA 98201
425-259-8849

Fox Island Historical Society
1017 Ninth Avenue
Fox Island, WA 98333
253-549-2461

Issaquah Historical Society
165 Southeast Andrews Street
Issaquah, WA 99027
425-392-3500

Jefferson County Historical Museum
210 Madison Street
Port Townsend, WA 98368
360-385-1003

Jefferson County Historical Society
210 Polk Street, Suite 11
Port Townsend, WA 93868
360-385-1003
www.jchsmuseum.org/

Kirkland Heritage Society
203 Market Street
Kirkland, WA 98033
425-827-3446

Northwest Seaport
1002 Valley Street
Seattle, WA 98102
206-447-9800

Orcas Island Historical Museum
P.O. Box 134
Eastsound, WA 98245
360-376-4849

Points N.E. Historical Society
201 Tulalip Street Northeast
Tacoma, WA 98422
253-943-9569

Puget Sound Mariner's Museum
3311 Harborview Drive
Gig Harbor, WA 98335
253-858-9395

Redmond Historical Society
16600 Northeast Eightieth Street
Redmond, WA 98052
425-885-2919

San Juan Historical Museum
P.O. Box 441
Friday Harbor, WA 98250
360-378-3949

Seattle Museum of the Mysteries
623 Broadway Avenue East
Seattle, WA 98102
206-328-6499

Snohomish County Museum
and Historical Association
2817 Rockefeller Avenue

Everett, WA 98201
425-259-2022

Snohomish Historical Society
118 Avenue B
Snohomish, WA 98290
360-568-5235

Steilacoom Historical Museum
112 Main Street
Steilacoom, WA 98388
253-584-4133

Tacoma Historical Society
3712 South Cedar Street #101
Tacoma, WA 98409
2563-472-3738

Washington State Historical Society
1911 Pacific Avenue
Tacoma, WA 98402
253-272-3500

Whatcom County Historical Society
P.O. Box 2116
Bellingham, WA 98225
www.whatcomhistory.net/wchs.html

Wing Luke Asian Museum
507 Seventh Avenue South
Seattle, WA 98104
206-623-5124

Index